The root of the Arab-Israeli conflict and the path to peace

Jaime Kardontchik

Introduction

The persecutions and pogroms suffered by the Jews in the Arab countries, from Northern Africa to the Middle East, before and during the 20ᵗʰ century, and the almost one million Jewish refugees from the Arab countries, have been ignored and deleted from the books and the conscience, both in the Western and in the Arab world.

My book corrects the wrong perspective, which focuses on the anti-Semitism in Europe in the 19ᵗʰ century and the first half of the 20ᵗʰ century, and ignores no less difficult conditions and persecutions that the Jews in the Arab countries went through at that time. Setting the record straight is not an arid intellectual exercise, since how the Arab world saw and behave towards the Jews in its midst for centuries, determined its view towards Zionism and the birth of the Jewish State in 1948. And the way that one sees the birth of the State of Israel in 1948 will shape his/her opinion of everything else related to the Arab-Israeli conflict today.

From Mecca in the Arabian Peninsula, and from the 7ᵗʰ century and on, Arabs began a conquest and colonization of vast territories, capturing the whole Middle East and North Africa. At the beginning of the 20ᵗʰ century, this Muslim-dominated world saw a mounting pressure for self-determination of non-Muslim minorities trapped in their midst, or – at a minimum – their desire to achieve basic equality of human rights. These aspirations were crushed. Examples abound: the Armenian and Assyrian genocides in 1915, the massacre of Assyrians in 1933 in Iraq, the persecution of Copts in Egypt. Only the Jews were able to fulfill their right to self-determination, but this right has been questioned by the Arab and Muslim world, through multiple wars, political isolation, and economic boycotts.

The history of the Arab-Israeli conflict is presented today, in the media and academia, mainly from the perspective of the Arab colonizers. This book presents the other side of the coin: the Jewish perspective of the conflict between the Jews and the Arabs.

***

The book comes in an English edition (which you have here) and also in a Spanish edition, titled "*La raíz del conflicto árabe-israelí y el camino hacia la paz*".

There is also a separate edition geared toward high-school teachers and students in the US, titled: "*Ethnic Studies in K12 schools: The Jewish module*".

For the general public, I recommend "*The root of the Arab-Israeli conflict and the path to peace*", in its English or Spanish editions.

The three editions are available at Amazon in eBook (Kindle, Tablet, Phone) and printed (paperback) formats.

Finally, there is a Hebrew edition of this book for people living in Israel, titled:

"הסכסוך הערבי-ישראלי"

Preface

This small book does not intend to deal with all the issues related to the Arab-Israeli conflict: it only concentrates on the basic issues of it. But I am convinced that once the reader understands the origin and essence of the conflict, then all the other pieces of the conflict can be understood and the path to true peace will be possible.

The audience for this book is general: Gentiles and Jews, Arabs and Israelis. The reader can be a student just starting high school or an adult. This great variety determined the style of the book and the form: a series of nine lessons or chapters, generously illustrated.

The first lesson explains the root cause of the Arab-Israeli conflict. The second lesson describes the social and political circumstances in Europe *and in the Arab countries* that fueled the mass migration of Jews at the end of World War II, giving rise to the birth of the State of Israel. The third lesson is a webinar by Dra. Einat Wilf, former political adviser to Nobel Peace Prize laureate Shimon Peres. It explains why all efforts to achieve peace between Israel and the Palestinians have failed so far. This webinar was organized by the Jewish Federation of Palo Alto, California, in April 2022. The fourth lesson provides a bird's eye view of the struggles of survival of non-Muslim minorities in the Middle East. The fifth lesson is a brief 5-page summary of 3,500 years of Jewish history, which also familiarizes people with terms such as "Sephardic, "Mizrahi," and "Ashkenazi" Jews. The sixth lesson is a round table with the participation of young leaders from the United Arab Emirates, Bahrain, Syria, Morocco and Israel, Jews and Arabs. This roundtable was organized by the Jewish Federation of Sacramento, California, in November 2021. The round table symbolizes the need for dialogue and inclusion to achieve real peace between Jews and Arabs. The seventh lesson is how I see a possible path for the resolution of the conflict. Lesson 8 refers to the massacre of Jews in Israel on October 7th, 2023, and the reaction of the Islamic world. Lesson 9, "The day after: Back to the 242", closes the book.

Jaime Kardontchik

Silicon Valley, California

March 2024

Contents

Lesson 1

"*Hebrea nací y Hebrea quero morir*" [*]

[*] "*I was born a Jew and I want to die a Jew*" (original words in Ladino, the common language spoken by Sephardi Jews)

Words said by **Sol Hachuel**, a seventeen Jewish girl, before being beheaded for refusing to convert to Islam.

City of Fez, Morocco, year 1834

The Islam doctrine and the Jews

Figure 1: President Biden at a press conference with South Korean president Moon Jae-in on May 21, 2021, responding to a reporter's question about the Israeli-Arab conflict. Recording time: 18:51 minutes.

"Let us get something straight here. Until the region says unequivocally that they acknowledge the right of Israel to exist as an independent Jewish state, there will be no peace". This was President Biden's straightforward response to a reporter's question following the latest conflagration between Israel and Hamas in May 2021.

The *Muslim* opposition to an independent Jewish State in the biblical Land of Israel (aka Palestine) is rooted in the religious teachings of Islam. Since the 7th century, as Arabs conquered vast lands in their expansion from Mecca, in Saudi Arabia, to the whole Middle East and the Mediterranean countries in Northern Africa, a doctrine was developed whose basic tenet was, and still is: *lands conquered by Muslims belong to the Umma* (the Islamic Community) *and cannot be surrendered. Never.* Non-Muslim residents in these lands can, at best, achieve the status of "*dhimmi*" – if they are *"People of the Book"* (Jews and Christians). Members of other religions were less fortunate: for them the options were conversion, expulsion or death.

The "*dhimmi*" status was formally bought by paying a special tax ("*jizya*") that granted personal security (protection from the mob) and basic religious autonomy in return for constant *submission*. Submission was expressed in a variety of ways. Dhimmis could not testify against a Muslim in a court of law. Murderers of dhimmis were rarely punished, as they could justify their acts by accusing the victims of blasphemy against

Islam. The case of a Pakistani Christian woman, Aasiya Noreen, is well known: In 2010 she was convicted of blasphemy by a Pakistani court and sentenced to death by hanging. Public degradation and humiliation of dhimmis was commonplace. At times and places, dhimmis were required to wear special badges (yellow for Jews) and were barred from riding horses, considered too noble for dhimmis, and restricted to using donkeys. The threat of violence, individual or collective, against "*dhimmis*" was always present, and oftentimes actually implemented as a reminder of their inferior status. Just to indicate a few modern events prior to the establishment of the State of Israel: In June 1-2 1941, a pogrom in Baghdad, *Iraq* (also known as the *Farhud* or *"violent dispossession"*), ended with over 180 Jews killed and around thousand Jewish homes destroyed. In November 5-7 1945, a pogrom started in Tripoli, **Libya**, and quickly spread to neighboring cities: at least 130 Jews were killed and hundreds of Jewish homes were pillaged or destroyed, including nine synagogues. In December 1947, in Aleppo, **Syria**, anti-Jewish riots resulted in some 75 Jews murdered and several hundred wounded. Ten synagogues were destroyed.

The "*dhimmi*" condition in the Islamic world, a state of constant legal, social and psychological submission, is often ironically hailed as an example of benign "*tolerance*" of the Islam towards the Jews.

Jews lived in the Middle East – and not only in the Land of Israel – well before the Arab conquest of these lands in the 7th century. The Jewish community in *Iraq* had existed for **2,500 years**, since the Babylonians conquered Jerusalem in 586 BCE and forcedly exiled the Jews to Iraq (then Babylonia). Jews lived in Aleppo and Damascus, **Syria**, for more than **2,000 years**. A large Jewish community lived in **Libya** for more than **2,000 years** (the Jewish revolt in Cyrenaica (Libya) against the Roman Empire in years 115-117 CE is well known.).

The Jewish communities in Iraq, Libya and Syria - 150,000 Jews – were eradicated in just three years, between 1949 and 1951, dispossessed and expulsed, ethnically cleansed. They were a civilian and defenseless minority. They were absorbed by Israel. And so was the fate of the Jews in **Yemen,** who lived there centuries before the birth of Islam: 50,000 Yemenite Jews were airlifted in 1949-1950 to Israel, after having endured the harshest aspects of Islamic "dhimmi" practices, including the forced conversion to Islam of Jewish minors, reimposed in the 1920's. In 1948 there were around 300,000 Jews in **Morocco**. Today, there remain only 2,000. Most of the Moroccan Jews sought refuge in Israel: The State of Israel is home today to about half a million Jews of Moroccan descent.

In the 20th century, in less than one-generation time, 870,000 Jews living in the Arab countries – from North Africa to the Middle East – were ethnically cleansed. *No one in the West wants to mention nor talk about the Jewish refugees from the Arab countries: it is a cause of discomfort and does not fit the predetermined ideological conceptions and frameworks.*

Jews are "dhimmis". *In the Western world every human being has inherent human rights.* **"Dhimmis" have no inherent human rights**: *they are given limited rights by the Muslim rulers at the rulers' discretion and these rights can be taken away at any time and place. Jews are expected to behave as "dhimmis", otherwise their fate is to* *be expelled or killed.* This doctrine is inculcated to children in the Islamic world, and what is taught to kids from young age is difficult to erase. It stays as such unchanged (*"the Hamas doctrine"*) or rationalized in or merged with Western-palatable ideologies (*"Israel as a colonial-settler enterprise"* or *"the right of return"*).

Recommended reading:

An account of the life of the Jews in Muslim lands since the times of the 7th century Arab conquest till modern times can be found in the book:

Martin Gilbert: *"In Ishmael's house: A history of Jews in Muslim lands"* (2010 edition)

Appendix 1.1: The Jews in Morocco at the end of the 19th century

Nomenclature:

Bilad al-siba: areas run by tribal authorities, generally rural and mountainous areas

Bilad al-makhzan: areas under central government control, generally centered around large towns or cities

For the fate of the Jews in the bilad al-makhzan, the urban centers, of Morocco, see Lesson 2, Appendix 2.1

Every Jew in the bilad al-siba belongs body and soul to his master, his sid. If the Jew's family had been established in the country for many years, then he belongs to the sid's property as an inheritance under the rules of Muslim law or Imazighen custom. If he had personally settled in the area where he now lived, then immediately upon arrival he must have been designated as 'someone's Jew'. Once this dependence is acknowledged, he and his posterity are forever bound to the master he had chosen. The sid protects his Jew against strangers as one would one's own property. He exploits him, as he pleases, as one would one's own estate. If the Muslim is astute and thrifty, he treats his Jew sparingly and takes no more than the interest on this 'capital' – demanding only an annual payment based on the season's profit. He is careful not to demand too much for he does not want to impoverish his Jew. On the contrary, he will facilitate his path to fortune, for the richer the Jew, the more profitable he is. He does not harass his family, nor appropriate his wife or daughter so that he does not try to escape enslavement by fleeing. In this way, the property of the sid increases from day to day, like a wisely administered farm.

If, however, the master is reckless and prodigal, he will use out his Jew like the squandering of an inheritance. Were he to demand of him exorbitant sums, the Jew would claim not to have them. The sid would then take his wife hostage, secluding her in his house until the Jew pays and then, before long, new demands would be made resulting in renewed brutality. The Jew leads the poorest and the most miserable existence, unable to earn a cent without it being wrested from him. Even his children are taken away from him, and finally he himself is led to the market-place, put up for auction and sold – as is practiced in certain parts of the Sahara but not everywhere. Or else he is ransacked, his home is destroyed and he and his family are driven away naked. Some villages can be seen were a whole quarter is deserted; the astonished passer-by learns that there was once a mellah [a Jewish quarter] there and that the sids had one day, by concerted action, stripped their Jews of everything and then evicted them.

Nothing on earth can protect a Jew against his master – he is at his mercy. If he wishes to absent himself temporarily, he must obtain the master's permission, which will not be withheld, since it is necessary for Jews to travel for trade purposes. But under no

circumstances whatsoever might he take his wife and children with him; his family must remain under the sid to guarantee his return. Were he to wish to marry his daughter to a stranger who would carry her off to his region, the fiancé would be compelled to purchase her from the master at any price the latter may see fit to demand. The ransom will vary according to the young man's fortune and the maiden's beauty. In Tikirt I saw a pretty Jewess who came from Warzazat. The husband paid 400 francs to be allowed to take her away, an enormous sum in a mellah where the richest man possesses a maximum of 1,500 francs.

However enslaved he may be, the Jew can free himself and leave the region if his sid gives him permission to ransom himself, but more often than not the sid turns down his request. If ever he does consent, it is because the Jew, as a result of business dealings, has held the better part of his fortune beyond the master's reach. In such a case the latter fixes the price of the ransom, either collectively for the whole family or individually, for each member of the family. The amount demanded is the greater part of the Jew's presumed wealth. Once the deal is concluded and the ransom paid the Jew is free. He moves out with his family unhindered and goes off to settle wherever he sees fit. If he does not wish to give the amount demanded or is unable to do so, or if all offers are deliberately rejected and he is nevertheless determined to leave at all costs, there remains but one option – to run away! Advanced preparations are made, carried out with the utmost secrecy. On a dark night he creeps out stealthily followed by his family, while all are asleep and, unseen, he proceeds to the village gate. Pack animals and an escort of Muslim strangers await him. They mount the animals, they leave, fleeing post-haste. Running at night, hiding during the day, avoiding inhabited places, choosing circuitous and forsaken routes, they quickly reach the edge of the 'bilad al-makhzan and there, at last, they can breathe easily. They are completely safe when they arrive in a big city.

The fugitive Jew is in mortal danger. As soon as the master hears of his escape, he sets out in pursuit of him and if he catches up with him, he slays him as he would a thief who had made off with his goods. If the escape is successful, the Jew and his descendants for several generations to come will avoid approaching his former place of residence even at a distance. He will keep at least three or four days' distance away and even then he will be worried. I have seen Jews of over fifty, whose father had run away from Mahamid al-Ghuzlan before they were born, consider as perilous for them to approach Tanzida and Mrimima, where they could, so they said, encounter Berabers and be captured by them. Wherever a sid finds his Jew or his offspring, he lays his hands on them. There are tales of Jews whose ancestors had run away and who, over eighty years later, where taken back in chains to the region of their ancestors by the descendent of their master.

This right sometimes gives rise to strange occurrences. Once, two rabbis from Jerusalem arrived in Dades to collect contributions. As they crossed the market-place a Muslim pounced on them crying, 'These are my Jews, I recognize them. Forty years ago, when they were young, they ran away with their father. At long last, Allah has restored them to me! Praised be to Allah!' The poor rabbis protested that their families had lived in Jerusalem for ten generations, they themselves had never left the Holy Land previous to this visit and wished to Heavens that they had never left at all! 'May

Allah curse your thief of a father! I swear that I recognize you and that you are my Jews'. Carrying them back to his region, he only agreed to free them for a price of 800 francs paid for them by the community of Tilit.

In the case of tribes that are democratically organized such as the Beraber for example, every Jew has a different master. In tribes governed by a despotic chief such as the Mezgita and the Tazderwalt, the Jews all belong to the sheikh and have no other sid but him. In places which a have a sheikh but whose authority is limited – in Tazenakht, among the Zenaga – the Jews must pay him an annual tribute, and may not move away without paying him a ransom. They belong nonetheless to a particular master who has common rights over them.

The region where I saw the Jews being the most mistreated and miserable, was in the Valley of Wad al-Abid, from Wawizert to Tabia. There I found Jewesses who had been sequestered by their master for three months because their husbands had not been able to pay up a certain sum. The local custom fines a Muslim 30 francs for the murder of a Jew. He owes them to the sid of the dead man and is given no other penalty or damage. In this region the Jews do not indulge in trade, for as soon as they earn anything it is snatched away from them. They cannot be jewelers through lack of capital and so they are all cobblers. Treated like animals, fate has turned them into wild and fierce creatures.

Excerpt from the book "**Reconnaissance au Maroc, 1883-1884**" by Charles de Foucauld, published in Paris in 1888, (English translation: Paul B. Fenton and David Littman, "Exile in the Maghreb", pages 270-273)

Charles de Foucauld (1858-1916) was a French soldier, explorer, geographer, ethnographer, Catholic priest and hermit who lived among the Tuareg (Imazighen) people in Northern Africa. He was canonized by the Catholic Pope Francis in 2022.

Lexicon

Bilad al: lands of

Imazighen (plural of *Amazigh*): inhabitants of Northern Africa before the Arab conquest of these regions (or their descendants), who converted to Islam.

Appendix 1.2: The Jews of Iran in the 19th century

1839: Persian Jews given choice: Convert or die

By **David B. Green**

[Published in the *Haaretz* newspaper, March 19, 2013]

March 19, 1839, is the date that the Jews of Mashhad, Persia [Iran] were given the choice of converting to Islam or dying, in an event that came to be known as the "Allahdad", meaning "God's Justice".

The ultimatum was preceded by an attack by an angry crowd on the neighborhood where the city's Jews resided, during which nearly 40 Mashhadi Jews were killed. Following that, the rest of their 2,400 or so brethren publicly accepted Islam – although most continued to practice their Judaism surreptitiously.

Jews had only resided in Mashhad – in the far northeastern corner of Persia, and today Iran's second-largest city – since 1746, when Nader Shah, the empire's king, moved his capital there and ordered 40 Jewish families to accompany him.

Mashhad was already a major object of Shi'ite pilgrimage and was known for the piety of its population, which did not welcome their new Jewish neighbors. Nonetheless, those Jews, who were confined to a ghetto-like neighborhood on the city's outskirts, created a community, developed trading ties with other towns in the region and eventually with their immediate neighbors too, and grew to some 200 families.

The Allahdad began, as such events usually do, when rumors began to spread that the city's Jews were mocking the Muslim religion, and on a holy day, no less.

The public appealed to their religious leaders, who turned to the town's political leader, who granted the crowd permission to vent their wrath on the Jews. They invaded the Jewish quarter, attacked homes and business, burnt books, and destroyed the synagogue. Thirty-six Jews lost their lives that day.

The physical violence was followed by the demand that the surviving Jews convert. The community capitulated to the demand and its members became "Jadid al-Islam" – new Muslims. They took on Arabic names, began to publicly embrace the rituals of Islam, including making the Hajj pilgrimage to Mecca.

At the same time, in a manner very similar to that of the crypto-Jews during the Spanish inquisition, they also secretly continued to live as Jews. They gave their children second, Hebrew, names, they fed the unkosher meat they openly bought to their animals and carried out shehita (kosher slaughter) surreptitiously. They also established clandestine synagogues in their basements.

They reproduced by hand the sacred Hebrew books that had been destroyed during the Allahdad, and used them to continue teaching their children Torah. They even found a way to avoid having their children intermarry with non-Jews, by marrying them off to other members of the community while they were still very young, age 9 or 10, so that when inquiries came from the city's Muslims, they could say their children were already spoken for.

Only after the ascent of Reza Pahlavi, the father of the last shah, to power, in 1925, and the start of a period of social liberalization, which included freedom of religion, did the crypto-Jews who still lived in Mashhad return to openly practicing their faith. That period lasted until 1946, when anti-Jewish riots erupted in Mashhad yet again. At that point, the city's Jews began to leave en masse. They went either to Tehran, where they constituted a distinct community, served by ten "Mashhadi" synagogues, or left Iran altogether.

Today, all the descendants of the Jews of Mashhad are outside their native land. Most can be found in Israel, and there is a large contingent in New York – in Kew Gardens, Queens, and in Great Neck.

***

Lexicon

Mashhad: city in northeast Iran

Shi'ite: an adherent of the Shia branch of Islam

Kosher: (of food, or premises in which food is sold, cooked, or eaten) satisfying the requirements of Jewish religious law.

Shehita: slaughtering of certain mammals and birds for food, following the rules of Jewish religious law

Torah: the first five books of the Hebrew Bible (Old Testament)

En masse: all together, as a group

Shah: king. A royal title that was historically used by the leading figures of Iranian monarchies

***

David B. Green is a longtime writer and editor at the Israeli newspaper Haaretz.

Additional reading:

Hilda Nissimi, "*Memory, Community, and the Mashhadi Jews during the Underground Period*", Journal of Jewish Social Studies, New Series, Vol 9, No 3 (Spring – Summer, 2003, pp. 76-106), Indiana University Press

https://www.jstor.org/stable/4467657

Hilda Nissimi is a Professor at Bar Ilan University, Israel

Appendix 1.3: The pogrom in Bagdad, Iraq, year 1941

"Farhud – violent dispossession – an Arabicized Kurdish word that was seared into Iraqi Jewish consciousness on June 1 and 2, 1941. As the Baghdadi Jewish communities burned, a proud Jewish existence that had spanned 2,600 years was abruptly incinerated.

As a nine-year old, I, Sabih Ezra Akerib, who witnessed the Farhud, certainly had no understanding of the monumental consequences of what I was seeing. Nevertheless, I realized that somehow the incomprehensible made sense. I was born in Iraq, the only home I knew. I was proud to be a Jew, but knew full well that I was different, and this difference was irreconcilable for those around me.

That year, June 1 and 2 fell on Shavuot – the day the Torah was given to our ancestors and the day Bnei Israel, the Sons of Israel, became a nation. The irony of these two historical events being intertwined is not lost on me. Shavuot signified a birth while the Farhud symbolized a death – a death of illusion and a death of identity. The Jews who had felt so secure, were displaced once again.

We had been warned trouble was brewing. Days earlier, my 20-year old brother, Edmund, who worked for British intelligence in Mosul, had come home to warn my mother, Chafika Akerib, to be careful. Rumors abounded that danger was coming. Shortly after that, the red hamsa (palm print) appeared on our front door – a bloody designation marking our home. But for what purpose?

Shavuot morning was eerily normal. My father Ezra had died three years earlier, leaving my mother a widow with nine children. I had no father to take me to synagogue, therefore, I stayed home with my mother, who was preparing the Shavuot meal. The rising voices from the outside were at first slow to come through our windows. However, in the blaze of the afternoon sun, they suddenly erupted. Voices – violent and vile. My mother gathered me, my five sisters and youngest brother into the living room, where we huddled together. Her voice was calming. The minutes passed by excruciatingly slowly. But I was a child, curious and impatient. I took advantage of my mother's brief absence and ran upstairs, onto the roof.

At the entrance of the open courtyard, at the center of our home, stood a 15-foot date palm. I would often climb that tree. When there was not enough food to eat, those dates would sustain us. I expressed gratitude for that tree daily. I now climbed that tree and wrapped myself within its branches, staring down at the scene unfolding below. What I saw defied imagination.

On the narrow dirt road, 400 to 500 Muslims carrying machetes, axes, daggers, and guns had gathered. Their cries – Iktul al Yahud, Slaughter the Jews – rang out as bullets were blasted into the air. The shrieks emanating from Jewish homes were chilling. I hung on, glued to the branches. I could hear my mother's frantic cries "Weinak! Weinak!" (Where are you?) But I could not answer, terrified of calling attention to myself.

Amidst the turmoil, I saw our landlord sitting by our door, wearing his distinctive green turban. He was a hajji, considered a holy man because he had made the mandatory pilgrimage (hajj) to Mecca, Saudi Arabia. Demanding, raging men were remonstrating with him, and then, inexplicably, they moved on. For some reason, our home was left undisturbed. Only later were we told that our landlord had explained to the men that a widow with nine children lived inside and had asked for his protection. Kindnesses abound when least expected, and for this I thanked G-d.

The horrors continued to unfold. The killing of men and children and attacks on Jewish women were rampant. Four doors down – at the home of Sabiha, my mother's good friend – a Muslim emerged carrying what appeared to be a bloodied piece of meat. We learned afterwards that Sabiha had been killed and mutilated. My mother's sorrowful refrain would later ring out: "Sabiha! They attacked her! They cut her throat! They mutilated her!"

At the same time, Jews were scampering over the roofs, running for their lives. If not for the looting taking place below, more would have been murdered. No authorities came to help; barbarism ruled. All the anger and jealously that had been pent up over centuries erupted in these horrific moments. Neighbors with whom we had shared a nod, a smile – and even attended their sons' circumcisions – had metamorphosed into sub-humans intent on annihilation.

And then, the fires started. Houses were being torched amidst the cries of their destroyers. Black smoke ascended towards the heavens. The putrid smell of smoke filled my nostrils – together with the smell of burning flesh. I will never forget those smells.

How long was I up there – one hour, two hours? I finally jumped down onto the roof, running into my mother's arms. Shaking, she slapped me – a slap of love.

We later learned that after leaving Dahana, these teeming masses of men, joined by others, went on to rampage the other impoverished neighborhoods, later making their way into the wealthier districts. The red hamsa signified their targets. All along Baghdad's main Rashid Street, Jewish shops that were closed for Shavuot were broken into and robbed. What the mob couldn't steal they destroyed. The multitude of synagogues lining the streets were equally ravaged – sifrei Torah [the books of the Bible] going up in smoke. The destruction was absolute and relentless.

On June 2, the second day of the Farhud, an eerie calm descended. Again, I ran upstairs and climbed the tree. In the distance were airplanes buzzing and bombs dropping. The British, who had camped on the outskirts of town as our communities burned, were finally moving into the city and reclaiming what had so tragically gone awry. But for the Jews of Baghdad this was too little, too late. What had been witnessed and experienced during those 24 hours would ring the death knoll for Iraqi Jewry. Many of us now understood that after 2,600 years, it was time to move on."

Source:

The personal story of the pogrom survivor, Steven Acre, was published in the AMI Magazine, August 3, 2011, and can be read in its entirety at:

https://www.mikecohen.ca/files/steve-acre-farhud-article.pdf

 A short video with Steve Acre describing the events can be seen at:

https://ms-my.facebook.com/USCSFI/videos/steve-acre-was-9-years-old-on-june-1-1941-when-armed-mobs-of-civilians-police-an/335358522048576/

Steve Acre was 9 years old on June 1, 1941, when armed mobs of civilians, police, and soldiers rampaged through Jewish neighborhoods ...

Appendix 1.4: The Egyptian Jews in the 1940's

*"A deep sudden yearning for a land of her own enveloped Inbar [a Jewish teenager]. Early in her life she had discovered that though she was born in Egypt and her family had been there for fifteen generations, because she was Jewish she could not obtain Egyptian nationality. Only 5 percent of the one hundred thousand Egyptian Jews had Egyptian nationality, the rest, though they had been born in Egypt, were either **apatride** – with no nationality – or had a foreign nationality from one of their ancestors.*

'So how did those 5 per cent obtain their Egyptian nationality?' Inbar asked her father once.

'These are mainly the very rich people, who obtained it through bribery', he responded sadly. 'Whenever I have applied for citizenship – and as you know, our family has been in Egypt for more than fifteen generations – I have been told that I would have to proof we have been here since the nineteenth century. But unfortunately, the Ottoman Empire, which ruled Egypt then, did not hold any registry of births in Egypt for the minorities, so it has been impossible to prove, and the authorities have known it all along. It was just a way to tell us we are not wanted as citizens, being Jews. We can stay here as 'welcomed guests', but not as citizens. We're dhimmi – the protected – but not equal.'

At school, Inbar sometimes watched with envy the Egyptian, English and French girls in the class. They have a country of their own, a culture of their own, a definite identity – not like me, she reflected with a sinking heart. Who am I? What am I? … I live in Egypt, yet I'm not an Egyptian. So, what am I?"

(Chapter 1, "*In the Shadow of the Pyramids*")

Excerpts from the book "***From the Nile to the Jordan***", by Ada Aharoni

Ada Aharoni – born in Cairo, Egypt – was a teenager when she was forced to leave Egypt with her family in 1949, with nothing else than one suitcase and twenty Egyptian pounds. Her father's license to work had been revoked and the family's assets confiscated. After a short period in France, Ada Aharoni emigrated to Israel in 1951.

Ada Aharoni is a writer and poet. She published 32 books, including historical novels, biographies, poetry collections and books for children. She has a PhD from the Hebrew University in Jerusalem. Ada Aharoni taught Literature at the University of Haifa, Israel, and at universities abroad, including the University of Pennsylvania.

The colonization of the mind

Email from a professor of History at a US university to the author (May 4, 2023):

"The vast majority of historical anti-Jewish violence occurred in Christian Europe. It cannot be equated to Arab-Islamic anti-Jewish violence (although this should not be ignored). You equate the two."

The author's reply (May 4, 2023):

I do not equate the two. The Holocaust is unique in History. In my book I do not refer to and not even mention the Holocaust.

The political Zionism emerged at the end of the 19th century, well before the Holocaust. At the end of the 19th century the situation of the Jews, the discrimination, persecutions and pogroms they suffered in Europe and in the Arab-Muslim countries were of similar intensity. In some respects, the situation of the Jews in some Arab countries was much worse, because their discrimination was institutionalized, legalized, and socially accepted and internalized by all, including both the Muslims and the Jews.

I will add here only a few words of the French historian Georges Bensoussan, from his book "*Jews in Arab countries: The great uprooting*" (published by Indiana University Press in year 2019):

"… This picture [the situation of the Jews in the Muslim countries at the end of the 19th century] can only be understood by accepting that it is the culmination of the long practice of dhimma, the protected status accorded to Jewish and Christian infidels, that was developed during Islam's first century. This long experience of submission fashioned a form of alienation difficult to render clearly discernable to those very people who internalized it. It became necessary to learn to survive within the tight confines of a domination that was neither the Hell some claimed, nor the Paradise that others said it was. It was an ordinary world in which codified violence kept everyone in his place, at the risk, otherwise, of bloodshed."

The situation of the Jews at the end of the 19th century in the vast Islamic lands extending from Morocco in the West to Iran and Yemen in the East, varied from place to place. It was worst in countries that lacked central governance, where local excesses were common and rarely scrutinized and reported by external observers. Access to these places were often difficult, but the occasional reports shared the same gloomy picture, as described earlier by Charles de Foucauld in year **1888**, regarding the situation of the Jews in the rural areas of Morocco, or the following description about the situation of the Jews in Iran, that appeared in a report by the French *Alliance Israelite Universelle*, in year **1903** (cited in Bensoussan's book, page 12):

"… Mistreated, chased like wild beasts, and systematically subjected to exceptionally harsh conditions, they have ended up resigned to their sad fate and they now find their situation entirely natural; they have become accustomed to lowering their heads while

the storm rages. Thus, any pride or dignity has disappeared, and ignorance has done the rest."

Or in some occasional notes about the Jews in Iran, that appear in the monumental book *"Persia and the Persian Question"* by Lord George N. Curzon, published in year **1892** (volume 1, page 510), written while he was working on a six-months assignment in Iran, as a correspondent for the London newspaper *Time*:

"Throughout the Mussulman countries of the East these unhappy people [the Jews] have been subjected to the persecution that custom has taught themselves, as well as the world, to regard as their normal lot. Usually compelled to live apart in a Ghetto, or separate quarter of the towns, they have from time immemorial suffered from disabilities of occupation, dress, and habits, which have marked them out as social pariahs from their fellow creatures."

This alienation of the Jew in the Muslim world, this internalization of the subjugation, was a unique experience of the Jews in the Muslim countries, not shared by the Jews in Europe. It was the colonization of their minds. In this sense, it was similar to the centuries-long experience of the Black people in the Southern states of the US. I categorize it as one of the worst forms of oppression.

***

Lexicon and note

Colonization of the mind: In sociology, a colonial mentality is the internalized attitude of ethnical or cultural inferiority felt by people as a result of colonization, that is, them being colonized by another group. It involves internalized negative views about oneself.

I shared a personal glimpse of this oppression, *"the colonization of the mind"*, in an article I published years ago. Here it is:

"… In 1981 I moved [from New Jersey] to Raleigh, the capital of North Carolina: I had gotten a job at the Physics Department of North Carolina State University. I still remember today the eerie feeling of sadness I felt when I first came to Raleigh and saw the rows of empty houses and a few black people walking with seemingly no purpose in the abandoned streets of the city …" ["In memory of Sandra Bland – A young black woman", published in the Jerusalem Post, July 27, 2015]

Lesson 2

Why the State of Israel came into being: Zionism and the birth of Israel

At the beginning of the 20th century anti-Semitism was rampant and Jews found themselves persecuted and unwanted everywhere. In the Arab world, from North Africa to the Middle East, the Jews suffered the chronic condition of "*dhimmis*", a status of legal, social and psychological submission to the Muslim majority accompanied by bursts of physical violence. On top of this, the surge of nationalism in the Arab countries found the Jews as an easy target for scapegoating, rioting and pogroms [see Appendix 2.1]. In Europe, anti-Semitism was deeply entrenched in the masses as a result of centuries of anti-Jew indoctrination and hatred spread by old Christian teachings and libels. Oftentimes the ruling classes incited the mobs against the Jews to provide a scapegoat for the misery of the masses. Discrimination was endemic and pogroms against the Jews were widespread [see Appendix 2.2].

A small group of Jewish intellectuals came to the conclusion that the problem needed a radical solution: the return of the Jews to *Zion* (the Land of Israel) and the reconstitution of the Jews as a normal people in their own land. A trickle of ideologically motivated Jews (the "*Zionists*") began returning to the Land of Israel, then a neglected far away province of the Ottoman Empire.

Life was extremely difficult for the Zionists: they came to the Land of Israel to become farmers, but swamps were usually the only places available for them. Diseases like malaria became common. They were poor and their previous experience in agricultural work was nil. They came up with an original solution: a system of collective socialist communes ("*kibbutzim*") was founded to survive and support each other. The first kibbutz, *Degania*, near the Sea of Galilee, was founded in 1910 by a group of ten men and two women:

Figure 1: Miriam Baratz tending cows at kibbutz Degania. Miriam was 21 when she joined a dozen men and women to found the kibbutz in 1910 (Photo from Wikimedia Commons)

https://jwa.org/encyclopedia/article/baratz-miriam

Other Zionists were more inclined towards a bourgeois lifestyle: On April 1909 several dozen families gathered on sand dunes next to the Mediterranean Sea and declared the foundation of a new neighborhood, which became with time the city of *Tel-Aviv*:

Figure 2: The founding of Tel-Aviv in 1909 (Photo from Wikimedia Commons)

In 1936, a mere 27 years after the founding of Tel-Aviv, the Israeli Philharmonic was born, giving its debut concert in Tel-Aviv under the direction of the legendary maestro Arturo Toscanini. Many of its musicians had just barely escaped the nightmare of Nazi Europe. The inaugural concert took place in an improvised under-construction "*concert-hall*":

Figure 3: Maestro Arturo Toscanini during the inaugural concert of the Israeli Philharmonic, in Tel-Aviv, December 1936, shaking hands with violinist Bronislaw Huberman, the founder of the orchestra (source: Felicja Blumental Music Center Library/Huberman Archive).

The Zionists were a small bunch of idealistic people in pursue of a dream.

Their dreams would not had become true if the worst of their nightmares would not had become a reality: the rise of Nazism – with hundreds of thousands of desperate Jews fleeing Europe – and the ethnic cleansing of the Jews in the Arab countries – with another half million Jews arriving to Israel from Northern Africa and the Middle East. America did its part, by closing its gates to immigration when the Jews most needed it.

Figure 4: In May 1939 the ship *St Louis* sailed from Hamburg, Germany, to La Habana, Cuba, carrying 937 passengers, most of them Jewish refugees. They had been given entry visas to Cuba, but upon their arrival to La Habana, Cuba's government refused to allow the ship to land. The ship continued to Miami, Florida. The passengers begged US President, Franklin D. Roosevelt, for sanctuary. They were refused. They also applied to land in Canada, but its prime minister refused. The ship went then back to Europe. More than two hundred of its Jewish passengers perished then in concentration camps. In 2012, the United States Department of State formally apologized to the survivors of the ship. In 2018, the Canadian prime minister Justin Trudeau issued a similar apology (Photo: United States Holocaust Memorial Museum)

On the eve of World War II, on May 23 1939, the British issued a policy statement known as the "*White Paper*". The new British policy limited the Jewish immigration to Palestine to 15,000 per year for the next five years (the official quota being 10,000 Jewish immigrants per year, leaving an additional 5,000 per year for special humanitarian circumstances). World War II was on the offing and the British Empire wanted the support of the Arab world. The European Jews got trapped inside Europe when they most needed an escape route.

Figure 5: Desperate attempts organized by the Jewish people to save Jews from Nazi Europe. One of them is shown in the photo above: In an illegal operation (in the eyes of the British), the ship *Parita*, carrying 850 Jewish refugees, lands on a sandbank off the Tel Aviv coast on August 1939 (Photo: United States Holocaust Memorial Museum). Many Jews who arrived illegally on Israel's shores during World War II were transported by English authorities to detention centers on the Mediterranean island of Cyprus. The British detained a total of some 50,000 Jewish refugees in these detention centers. Approximately 2,000 children were born there and around 400 people died during their internment. Finally, in 1949, with the end of English rule and the establishment of the State of Israel, the detention centers were closed and the refugees were received by Israel.

November 29, 1947: UN partition resolution 181

On that day, the United Nations General Assembly approved the partition of the land between the Jordan River and the Mediterranean Sea into two states, a Jewish State and an Arab State. The Jews accepted the UN resolution. The Arabs rejected it. A few hours later, pogroms against the Jews irrupted in the streets of Aleppo, Syria, and Aden, southern Yemen, as a warning message and presage of what would happen to the Jews in the Arab countries, if the Jews in Palestine dared follow up with the UN resolution and proclaim an independent Jewish state. [See Appendices 2.3-4]

Or, in the words of Dr Heykal Pasha, the representative of Egypt at the Ad Hoc Committee of the UN on Palestine during the November 24 1947 session, before the final vote on the partition resolution: *"Would the members of the UN place in certain and serious danger a million Jews in the Arab countries, simply in order to save a hundred thousand in Europe or to satisfy the Zionist dream?"*, adding that *"the Egyptian delegation was giving the world fair warning."*

May 14, 1948: Israel declares independence

With the British gone, the Jews declared independence in May 1948. The gates of Israel were finally opened for a massive influx of Jewish refugees from Europe and the Arab countries. **Jews in dire distress had finally a place where they could go to and be unconditionally accepted**.

The Independence War

The Arab states did not accept Jewish independence and invaded the nascent state. The situation was initially quite bad for the Jews and no one expected them to win the war. On the first night of Israel's Independence, Egyptian planes bombed Tel-Aviv. In just one of the frequent air bombings of Tel-Aviv, on May 18 1948, a 50-pound fragmentation bomb killed 41 and wounded an additional 60 persons. Women and children were among the 41 killed when the crowded Tel Aviv *bus terminal* was strafed [1]. A few weeks before, in April 1948, a convoy of nurses, doctors and medical students set out for the Hebrew University, located on Mount Scopus, Jerusalem. They were assaulted by Arab militia: 75 Jews perished in the attack. In May 1948, four *kibbutzim* in Gush Etzion, next to Jerusalem, were completely destroyed and about 130 Jews – who had surrendered – were summarily executed, women and men.

It was a bloody war that extended for a whole year.

Jews had nowhere to flee, so they stayed put, fought, and got their State.

***

Reference

[1] Associated Press, reported in the May 20, 1948, edition of *The Palestine Post* newspaper.

Note: The word *"strafed"* was used in *The Palestine Post* report. The word means *"attacked repeatedly with bombs or machine-gun fire from low-flying aircraft"*.

The ethnic cleansing of the Jews from the Arab countries

In less than one-generation time, about 870,000 Jews were expelled from the Arab countries, their properties confiscated and converted into refugees. The majority of these Jewish refugees were absorbed by Israel, as shown in the map below:

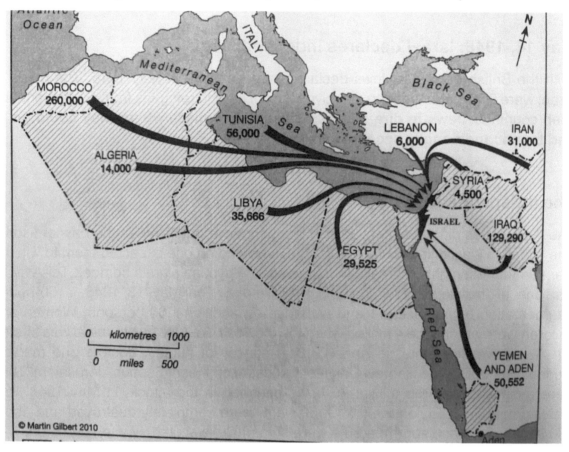

Figure 6: The numbers in the map show the number of Jews who were expelled from each Arab country and sought refuge in Israel between 1948 and 1972. Iran (not an Arab country) recognized Israel in 1950: 25,000 Jews from Iran emigrated to Israel in 1950-1951 (source: Martin Gilbert, "*In Ishmael's House: A history of Jews in Muslim lands*", 2010 edition)

The above map and the numbers cannot convey the scope of the tragedy of the Jewish refugees from the Arab lands. The massive ethnic cleansing of the Jews from the Arab countries has been systematically hidden and erased from the public memory in the Western world.

Figure 7: Yemenite Jews airlifted to Israel in 1949-1950 (Photo from Wikipedia Commons)

Between June 1949 and September 1950, 50,000 Yemenite Jews were airlifted to Israel, closing more than 2,000 years of Jewish life in the Arab peninsula. In Yemen, some of the harshest aspects of Islamic dhimmi practices had been reimposed in 1922, including the rule that Jewish children who became orphans before they were fifteen were forcibly converted to Islam [Ref 1, pages 157-158]. The airlift of the Yemenite Jews in 1949-1950 was preceded by riots: in Aden, at the Southern tip of Yemen, a Muslim mob attacked the Jewish Quarter in December 1947: 82 Jews were killed and 106 Jewish-owned shops were destroyed. A synagogue and Jewish schools were burned to the ground [Ref 1, pages 209-210].

"In Yemen, a nineteenth-century decree for the forcible conversion of Jewish orphans was reintroduced in 1922. The conversion of a **dhimmi** *orphan to Islam had always been considered a meritorious act. This followed the belief that every child, whoever his parents, was born into the* **fitra**, *or innate disposition, which was taken to mean that he was born a Muslim. ... For seven years the decree was rigorously implemented. When it was re-promulgated in December 1928, twenty-seven Jewish orphans were forced to convert to Islam within four months.*

On 3 January 1929 [in] the capital of Yemen, Sanaa, ... two young orphans, brother and sister, agreeable looking, were snatched away from their mother in full view of the Jewish population, despite the cries of the desperate family. The Jews got together and collected a sum of money in order to buy back the children. But this was in vain. The Quran prohibits Muslims from accepting money in order to prevent a conversion."

(From Martin Gilbert's book, pages 157-158)

Figure 8: Iraqi Jews airlifted to Israel in 1951 (Photo by Teddy Brauner, Government Press Office, Israel)

Decades long persecution of the Iraqi Jews culminated in 1951. In that year, 130,000 Iraqi Jews were airlifted to Israel. The Iraqi government stripped the Jews of their Iraqi citizenship as a condition for allowing them to leave the country. Then, the Iraqi Parliament secured the passing of a law whereby the assets of all the Jews who renounced Iraqi citizenship were frozen and put under the Iraqi government control. 2,500 years of Jewish life in that piece of land, since the times of the Babylonian Empire – and preceding by thousand years the Arab conquest in the 7th century CE – came to an abrupt end.

Israel was born as a nation of refugees, who came to its shores because they had nowhere else to go. They came with nothing, except for their bare hands and traumatized minds.

Reference

[1] Martin Gilbert: "*In Ishmael's house: A history of Jews in Muslim lands*" (2010 edition)

Further reading:

Carole Basri, *"The Jewish Refugees from Arab Countries: An Examination of Legal Rights – A Case Study of the Human Rights Violations of Iraqi Jews"*, Fordham International Law Journal, Volume 26, Issue 3, 2002:

https://ir.lawnet.fordham.edu/ilj/vol26/iss3/6/

(The paper can be downloaded for free)

Appendix 2.1: The Jews of Morocco caught between the French and the Arabs

I casually opened Martin Gilbert's book *"The Atlas of Jewish History"*. On page 80 there is a map titled "The Jews of Morocco". Part of it is shown below:

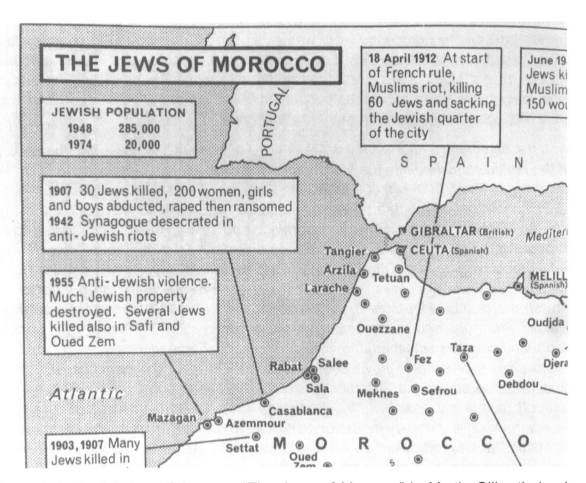

Figure A.1: Partial view of the map "The Jews of Morocco" in Martin Gilbert's book *"The Atlas of Jewish History", 1993*

The map shows the towns where Jews lived in Morocco. Small inserts indicate some painful events, many of them occurring at the beginning of the 20th century: pogroms in Debdou (1875), Taza (1903), Settat (1903, 1907), Casablanca (1907), Fez (1912). One caught my curiosity: it happened in *Casablanca*, a city well known in the West (at least since the movie by the same name, from 1942, starred by Humphrey Bogart). An insert laconically reads:

"1907: 30 Jews killed, 200 women, girls and boys abducted, raped then ransomed".

A quick search using Google gave me the following eyewitness account [1]:

***"1907 Cataclysmic destruction and pillage of Casablanca Mellah** [Jewish quarter]"*

On 1 August, a band of about 100 Kabyles [a Berber ethnic group centered mainly in North Africa] helped by some Arabs from the town, attacked the port dock-yard, derailed a small train, killed nine Europeans, and destroyed a large part of the installations. An immediate panic spread in the town; it was a premonition of things to come. Tuesday and Wednesday were days of indescribable suspense …

The [French] cruiser 'Galilee' appeared offshore on Thursday, 3 August. Its arrival spread a little calm in the town and until the following Tuesday, the situation seemed less alarming … Suddenly it changed. In the night of Monday to Tuesday, because either the 'Galilee' had received the order to bombard the town or because Moulai-Amin, the uncle of the Sultan, feeling overwhelmed, asked the protection from the French cruiser, the Europeans were warned at two in the morning to go in haste to their Consulates. At 5 am a picket of 75 sailors disembarked. You know the sequel: the Makhzen's [Moroccan] soldiers fired on them; they [the French sailors] crossed the town leaving a number of corpses behind them, arrived at the French consulate and gave the signal for the bombardment to commence.

With the first cannon shot, as if the Arabs were only waiting for this sign, the soldiers of the Makhzen rushed into the Mellah, followed by the whole population, and started the pillage. The 5,000 to 6,000 men who were waiting at the gates penetrated the town, spread out thorough the Mellah [the Jewish quarter] and the Medina [the city], robbing, looting, raping, killing and burning, and during three days sowed terror throughout the town, until the French troops disembarked. Not a house, not a family, not a person was spared. There are only five to six Jewish houses that remained intact because they were situated near the consulates. The Kaiseria, the quarter of the Jewish merchants, with more than 500 shops, was burned down; nothing but ruins remain. From one end to the other, without any exception, the Mellah was sacked: doors and windows smashed, furniture and contents gone; all has been cleaned out, demolished; our schools have been reduced to pieces; the benches and desks smashed, the equipment, the money stolen, the books burnt. At the Talmud-Tora [school], where my assistant, Mr. Soussana lived, everything was destroyed. Mr. Soussana was very ill: they took everything away from him, even his mattress and his nightshirt; he was left naked on his iron bedstead … all the synagogues, except for two small oratories, have been sacked, the silver stolen and the hekal (altar) desecrated. To the honor of our co-religionists, the sepharim [Scrolls of the law] were saved. Everywhere there is desolation and devastation. One wouldn't believe that men could have destroyed so much, but rather that the city had been the victim of a cataclysm.

But the looting, the fire is nothing. Chased out of their homes, the Jews scattered in all directions, around the precincts of the consulates, particularly the French consulate. There were battles between the Arabs and Europeans besieged in their consulates. Suffering heavy loses, the Arabs fell on the weakest: the Jews. A veritable man-hunt began. The Jews hid themselves in caves, under rubble, in empty tanks. Families lived for three days under straw, without food. The men were pursued and beaten with truncheons or stabbed; the women raped when there was time, or abducted with their children. Horrible scenes took place. The narrative from the mouths of the victims themselves is hair-rising …

Following my three-day investigation, I have made the following estimate which the authorities consider is most probably correct: 30 dead, some 60 wounded, of which 20 seriously; an unlimited number of rapes (I dare not question the families nor would they dare to admit it), more than 250 young women, girls, children abducted ...

Letter (15.8.1907) from Isaac Pisa, head of the Casablanca Boys' school to the President of the Alliance Israelite Universelle, AIU, Paris.

Note:

Alliance Israelite Universelle, AIU: A Paris-based Jewish organization founded in 1860 to safeguard the human rights of Jews around the world. It became particularly active in promoting education by funding Jewish schools and teachers throughout the Muslim world. In its origin, it was a non-Zionist organization promoting the integration of Jews in their countries of residence.

Reference

[1] David Littman, "*Jews under Muslim Rule – II: Morocco 1903-1912*", reprinted from The Wiener Library Bulletin, 1976 vol XXIX, New Series Nos 37/38 by the Eastern Press Ltd., London and Reading

The events in Casablanca and the pogrom on the Jews were also reported by the US newspapers. On August 9, 1907, the heading of "*The Herald Democrat*", a Colorado newspaper, reads "***Casablanca Lies in Ruins – Moors Pillage Jew Quarters***", and the report begins with a short description of the pogrom:

The Herald Democrat, August 9, 1907 iii/

<Previous issue | Next issue>

CASABLANCA LIES IN RUINS

Moors Pillage Jew Quarters

Tangier, Aug. 8.—The French warships have landed 2,000 extra men at Casablanca to stop the street fighting that is still going on. The Jewish quarters have been sacked and many persons in the streets of the city have been massacred,

Appendix 2.2: Pogroms against the Jews in Eastern Europe at the beginning of the 20th century

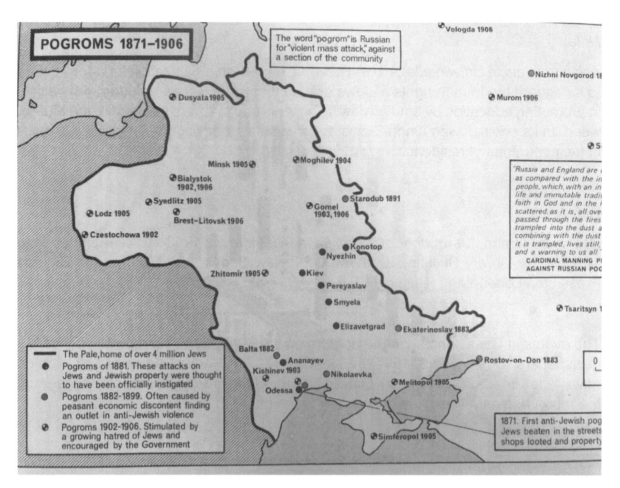

Figure A.2: Partial view of the map "Pogroms 1871-1906" in Martin Gilbert's book "*The Atlas of Jewish History*", 1993 (page 75). Date next to a city name indicates the year were a large pogrom occurred in that city.

Due to the present war in Ukraine, you can easily identify some cities in the map: Minsk (the capital of Belarus), Kiev (Kyiv, the capital of Ukraine), Kishinev (Chisinau, the capital of Moldova), Odessa (the main port city of Ukraine). These are all cities where pogroms were perpetrated against the Jews between 1871-1906. The pogroms were quite widespread: they included also cities like Lodz (Poland) in the West, Rostov-on-Don (Russia) in the East and Simferopol (Crimean Peninsula) in the South. They were all included in "*The Pale*" (marked on the map by a thick black borderline), the region of the then imperial Czarist Russia where Jews were restricted to live.

The Kishinev pogrom (1903)

According to official figures, 51 were reported dead – 49 of them Jews – and 74 seriously wounded. Horrifying eyewitnesses of rapes were reported. More than 1,500 shops and houses were plundered or destroyed.

The horrors and destruction in Kishinev were no different from what had happened in other cities at that time, in Odessa (1871), Kiev (1881), Minsk (1905) and in many other towns in Eastern Europe. *The difference was in the reaction of the Jewish intellectuals.* The Jewish poet Haim Bialik was at the scene of the slaughter in Kishinev. With the scenes still fresh in his mind he wrote (in Hebrew) and published weeks later his now famous poem "*In the city of slaughter*". The long poem begins with:

קום לך-לך אל עיר ההריגה ובאת אל החצרות,

ובעיניך תראה ובידך תמשש על הגדרות

ועל העצים ועל האבנים ועל-גבי טיח הכתלים

את הדם הקרוש ואת המוח הנקשה של החללים.

Arise and go to the city of slaughter, into its courtyards,

And with your eyes you will see and with your hand you will touch on the fences,

And on the trees and on the stones and on the painted walls,

The clotted blood and dried brains of the dead.

But then Bialik goes on in his poem into a sharp criticism of the past passivity of the Jews, who had accepted for generations this suffering in silence and calls them to take their destiny in their own hands, instead of letting others mold their lives.

ועצרתי את עיניך – ולא תהיה דמעה,

והקשחתי את לבבך – ולא תבוא אנחה.

I will let no tear fall from your eyes,

I will make hard your heart and will not permit a sigh.

ולמה זה יתחננו אלי? – דבר אליהם וירעמו!

ירימו-נא אגרוף כנגדי ויתבעו את עלבונם,

את עלבון כל-הדורות מראשם ועד סופם,

ויפוצצו השמיים וכיסאי באגרופם.

And why would they beg me [God]? Speak to them and they will roar!

Raise a fist against me and let them demand a retribution for the shamed,

The shame of all the generations, from the first to the last,

And the sky will explode and my chair will crumble under their fist.

Appendix 2.3: The pogrom in Aleppo, Syria, December 1947

"In November 1947, the United Nations issued its "Partition Plan for Palestine", calling for a complicated division into a separate Jewish state and the Arab state of Palestine. Arabs throughout the Middle East and North Africa went on rampages in protest. With historical perspective, many observers now conclude that these were not spontaneous eruptions of rage but rather mass insurgencies orchestrated by the Arab governments and police forces.

Mobs estimated at up to a hundred thousand people stormed Aleppo's Jewish quarter for days, breaking windows and destroying Jewish-owned business and homes. My grandparents hid in the basement with their children Margo, Ralph, Joe, Morris, and Edgar. When they heard a crowd of rioters break into the house, they snuck out and ran to the Armenian neighborhood, where a Christian man whom my grandfather knew through business gave them refuge for a few days until the hostilities ebbed.

My father's brother Joe, who was twelve years old at the time, told me: "When they divided Palestine to grant the State of Israel, Arabs in Syria revolted against those decisions and against the Jews. They went to every shul [Jewish school], every place they knew of as a Jewish congregation, and they took everything out of it and burned it – the Torahs [Bible], the prayer books, everything. Our house was in the center of town. We were the only people (in the neighborhood) that had a one-family house, and it was very well known that it was a Jewish family that owned it. Our house was one of the only family houses that were burned in that neighborhood. As they were burning everything, they went into the house, took the drapes, dipped them in gasoline and burned them."

When the rampage ended, the Armenian man whose family they were staying with went to the house to assess the damage. Though the house had not burned to the ground, it was damaged enough to be temporarily uninhabitable. My grandparents and their five children salvaged some belongings and moved in with their mother's sister Eugenie and her family in another part of town, sharing her small apartment for five or six months while their home was being repaired.

Dozens of Jews in Aleppo were killed in the riots, and more than two hundred Jewish homes, shops, and synagogues were destroyed – including my grandparents' neighborhood synagogue and the adjoining school that my father had attended and where his younger siblings now studied."

[Excerpts from the book "***Farewell, Aleppo***" by **Claudette E. Sutton**, 2014]

Claudette E. Sutton is a writer and editor. She lives in Santa Fe, New Mexico, USA. "*Farewell, Aleppo*" is the captivating story of her father and his family, Jews who had lived in Aleppo, Syria, from time immemorial.

Appendix 2.4: The pogrom in Aden (Yemen), December 1947

Jews of Aden recall the pogrom sparked by UN vote on Palestine Partition plan

By **Ofer Aderet**

[Published in the *Haaretz* newspaper on November 30, 2016]

"It's terrible to make this comparison, but fewer people were killed in the Kishinev pogroms than were killed in Aden. Perhaps if we'd had a Bialik, our memory would look different."

Figure A.3: Arabs set alight a Jewish school for boys in Aden, Yemen, during a demonstration against the UN partition of Palestine, on December 19, 1947. Credit: AP

Shimon Sasson, 84, of Tel Aviv, was 15 when the riot broke out in the port city of Aden. It happened just after November 29, 1947, the date in which the United Nations approved the partition plan for Palestine, paving the way for the founding of the State of Israel.

Shimon Sasson (credit: Tomer Appelbaum)

"I heard the report on the UN vote on the radio with my family at home in Aden," Sasson told Haaretz this week. *"Afterword we went downstairs and told everyone who'd*

gathered outside the house who had voted for [at the UN General Assembly], who against, and who had abstained. There was cheering."

But the joy was premature and replaced very shortly with alarm. *"What happened was totally unexpected and hit us out of nowhere,"* wrote Ovadia Tuvia, a Jewish Agency representative, describing the pogrom against local Jews to his superiors in Eretz Israel.

Today, November 30, Israel observes the Day to Mark the Departure and Expulsion of Jews from the Arab Countries and Iran, an official Memorial Day established by the Knesset two years ago.

In Aden, which at the time was a British colony and today is part of Yemen, there was an ancient community of Jews numbering around 5,000 people, who lived alongside the local Arab population. The rioting began on December 2, 1947 and lasted three days. *"On the night of December 2, the Arabs started to burn Jews' cars in the street,"* Sasson recalled. *"The next day they invaded our neighborhood. The streets were totally empty. We threw bottles at them."*

A day later Arabs started to torch Jewish stores, businesses, and homes. *"A few families fled their homes and ran to our house, which was in the middle of the neighborhood. I opened the door and took in five families,"* whose names he still remembers.

The Jewish leaders asked the British for help. In response, they sent a unit of Bedouin policemen under British command. *"That's when the disaster started,"* Tuvia wrote. *"The hooligans started to loot Jewish stores. The policemen stood aside and smiled. Another minute and you could see them assisting in the looting and pillaging."*

The British declared a curfew. *"I didn't know what a curfew was, so I went up on the roof to see what was happening in the street. I saw a soldier there with a rifle. I ducked and he shot at me."* The bullet didn't hit him, but hit a 15-year-old girl who had found refuge in his house. *"The bullet hit her in the head. She died on the spot,"* he said. *"There was great turmoil in the house."* They had to wait three days until they could put the body out for burial in a collective grave.

"Any Jew who called out for help or who went up to the roof to put out the fires in his house or to escape it was greeted with a hail of bullets," wrote Tuvia, who had been born in Aden in 1920, immigrated to Palestine and returned in 1945 to organize Aliyah to the soon-to-emerge state. *"The mad cries in the Jewish neighborhood tore the heavens. All the Jewish homes were pockmarked with bullet holes. One house was burned. Dozens of bodies fell, one after the other."*

Gavriel David, who was an infant at the time, lost his grandfather, Yihye, in the riots. His recollections are based on the stories he heard from relatives. *"Eighty-seven Jews were shot, slaughtered and burned to death. My grandfather was shot in the head by a sniper,"* he said. *"He didn't die on the spot. He bled all night at home."* Yihye was evacuated to a hospital the next day, but died of his wound.

After three days, when the British army finally came into the Jewish quarter, the rioting stopped. *"On Friday morning they went out to collect the dead,"* Tuvia wrote. *"A truck went from street to street to collect them. Every home brought down its dead to the middle of the street and Yemenite refugees buried them in a collective grave, with no funeral and no ceremony. The streets were filled with crying and wailing."*

Thirty days after the riots the Aden Jewish Association in Eretz Yisrael held a memorial for those murdered, in the community's synagogue at 5 Lilienblum Street in Tel Aviv. There, the community issued a call for the Jewish Agency and the country's institutions to do all in their power to bring Aden's Jews to the holy land.

Five years ago, a small museum was set up in the synagogue to document the community's history; it contains testimonies, documents, artifacts and photographs. One corner of the museum is dedicated to the pogrom. A memorial pamphlet lists the names of the 87 people killed in the rioting.

"The Aden community lost 87 people because of the declaration of the Jewish state. Their only sin was the founding of the State of Israel," said Sasson. A few months after the state was declared, he made Aliyah alone. His mother, who was heavily pregnant, and his sisters joined him afterward. His father remained in Aden until 1967, when the British withdrew from the territory.

There were those left behind in Aden, Sasson said. *"Not everyone hurt during the disturbances was located in the end,"* he said. *"There were those who disappeared and were never found. To this day we don't know where they are."*

Prof. Michael David, director of the Skin Department at Beilinson Hospital, and the brother of Gavriel David, is angry at the state for not preserving the memory of those murdered in the disturbances.

"When they mark November 29 in schools, they don't talk about this pogrom, which was directly connected," he said. *"It's terrible to make this comparison, but fewer people were killed in the Kishinev pogroms than were killed in Aden. Perhaps if we'd had a Bialik, our memory would look different,"* he said, referring to Haim Nahman Bialik's famous poem, "In the City of Slaughter," written after the Kishinev pogroms in 1903.

***

Lexicon

Bialik: Jewish poet, who witnessed the pogrom in Kishinev (today the capital of Moldova, next to Ukraine, in Eastern Europe) and wrote a poem, *"In the City of Slaughter"*, in memory of the slaughtered Jews.

The Jewish Agency: An organization founded in 1929 to promote the immigration to Israel

Aliah: Hebrew name for immigration to Israel

Eretz Israel: Hebrew name for the Land of Israel (aka Palestine)

Knesset: the name of the Israeli Parliament

Beilinson Hospital: a hospital in central Israel

Lesson 3

"The war of return"

The Israeli-Arab Conflict

Seminar by Dr Einat Wilf

Editor: Jaime Kardontchik

Preface

The Congregation Beth Am of Los Altos Hills, and the Jewish Community Center of Palo Alto, both in the Silicon Valley, California, hosted on April 10, 2022, a 40-minutes Seminar with Dr Einat Wilf titled "*The Essence of the Israeli-Palestinian Conflict and the Path to Lasting Peace*". The Seminar was followed by a 40 minutes Q&A session. The video of the Seminar and the following Q&A is available at:

https://vimeo.com/699880975

The clarity of the ideas presented in this Seminar is outstanding. Hence, I decided to transcript it in writing, to reach wider audiences. My transcription is based on the original video. I apologize for any omissions and mistakes that I could have generated during the transcription.

About Einat Wilf:

Born and raised in Israel, Dr Wilf was a former policy advisor to Shimon Peres, a Nobel Peace laureate. She was a member of the Israeli parliament from 2010 to 2013, where she served as the Chair of the Education Committee and a member of the influential Foreign Affairs and Defense Committee. Dr. Wilf earned a B.A. from Harvard, an MBA from the INSEAD institute in France and a PhD in political science from the University of Cambridge, and she served as the Goldman Visiting Professor at the Georgetown University.

Jaime Kardontchik, PhD (Physics)

Silicon Valley, California

April 22, 2022

Introduction

Rabbi Jeremy Morrison

Congregation Beth Am

Good morning, and it is great that you have all joined us today. As the senior rabbi of Congregation Beth Am, it gives me great pleasure to welcome Einat Wilf as our speaker this morning. She will be talking to us from Israel about the Israeli-Palestinian conflict and the path to lasting peace. I want to thank the Beth Am Jewish and Israel advocacy committee and the Oshman Family Jewish Community Center for co-sponsoring today's program. I also want to thank Congregation Kol Emet, Congregation Beth Ami and the Jewish-Israeli Advocacy Committee [JIAC] for their contributions to this event.

Jeff Carmel

Beth Am JIAC

Thank you, Rabbi. As Rabbi Morrison mentioned, today's program is brought to you by Beth Am's Jewish and Israeli Advocacy Committee, whose mission is to mobilize support for the security of the State of Israel, to counter the alarming growth in anti-Semitism and promote respect for Jews in the United States and beyond. To this end, we educate congregants through emails and inspirational speakers, such as Dr. Wilf, as well as to provide timely alerts to take action as events warrant.

Born and raised in Israel, Dr Wilf served as an intelligence officer in the Israeli Defense Forces and was a former policy advisor to [Vice Prime Minister] Shimon Peres. She was a member of the Israeli parliament from 2010 to 2013, where she served as the Chair of the Education Committee and a member of the influential Foreign Affairs and Defense Committee. Academically, Dr. Wilf earned a B.A. from Harvard, an MBA from the prestigious INSEAD institute in France and a PhD in political science from the University of Cambridge, and she served as the Goldman Visiting Professor at the Georgetown University.

Most importantly, she is without doubt one of Israel's most articulated, thoughtful, lucid and captivating speakers on the Israeli-Palestinian conflict and the moral issues that arise from it. Having heard Einat speak on numerous occasions, I guarantee that by the end of today's webinar, we will all have a far better understanding of the conflict, its sources and its possible solutions.

Einat, on behalf of the more than three hundred and fifty registrants for today's program: *Welcome!*

Einat Wilf

Thank you so much for having me. Thank you for this kind introduction, and I promise that what I am going to do today is let you know what the conflict is all about and how to solve it. That's it. You will be done and you will know.

I want to share with you a little bit as to how I even began to think about the conflict, my personal journey and how I came to the conclusions that I am going to share with you. I grew up in Israel, I grew up in Jerusalem. I was very much part of what politically is traditionally known in Israel as the Israeli Left, Israeli's Peace Camp, a member of the Israeli's Labor Party. As a young adult I voted for [Prime Minister] Itzhak Rabin, later for [Prime Minister] Ehud Barak, and as a member of the Israeli Peace Camp, I very much supported what through the eighties and the nineties was the *main idea* associated with the Israeli Peace Camp, which was this very simple equation known as "*Land for Peace*". The idea of this simple equation was that Israel has a path to peace and the path to peace is based on "*Land for Peace*" as a formula. Which land? The land that Israel captured as the result of the Six Day 1967 war: the Sinai Peninsula in the South, the Golan Heights in the North, and the West Bank and the Gaza Strip in the center.

Why was it necessary to come up with this formula? As I am sure you know, after Israel was established, after the war of 1948-1949, *none* of Israel's neighbors was willing to make peace with it. All what Israel's neighbors were willing to do was to sign *cease fire* agreements. So, when people speak about the pre-1967 borders, there were never any borders: those were *cease-fire* lines, which the Arab countries surrounding Israel – Lebanon, Syria, Jordan and Egypt – made clear that they were cease fire lines in an ongoing war. The message was that the battle of 1948-1949 may be over momentarily or temporarily, but basically this is a cease fire in a far bigger and ongoing war of these Arab states, Arab countries, against the establishment of the Jewish state of Israel.

So, Israel had no peace when it was born. But after the really amazing victory in 1967 and the capture of all these lands, which really tripled the size of Israel, just as you get a sense of the proportion, the sense was that Israel has now territorial assets that it can exchange for peace with its Arab neighbors.

For a while the "*land for peace*" seemed to be a very successful formula. This was the basis for the peace agreement with Egypt, Israel's largest foe. Basically, Israel signed a peace agreement with Egypt and in exchange gave Egypt the Sinai Peninsula that was more than twice the size of Israel. We can have a very interesting discussion as to whether what we have or had with Egypt was peace, but we officially signed with Egypt a peace agreement and handed over the entirety of the territory of the Sinai Peninsula.

The ninety nineties were really a decade for the "land for peace" formula. This was also the decade of the Rabin government and of Ehud Barak. We negotiated with Syria over the Golan Heights, we signed a peace agreement with Jordan, when Jordan gave up its territorial claims to the West Bank, and, of course, the highlight of the nineties were the Oslo Accords, where Israel negotiated directly with the Palestinians, with the Palestinian Liberation Organization, with Yasser Arafat, with the Palestinians, over the future of the West Bank and Gaza.

The ninety nineties come to a pinnacle in the year 2000, when Ehud Barak – the head of the Labor party, the head of the Israeli Peace Camp – goes to Camp David. Camp David is symbolic: this is where Israel negotiated the peace agreement with Egypt. He goes to Camp David to meet with Arafat and to negotiate a final peace agreement over the future of the West Bank and Gaza. When Ehud Barak – who was clearly elected on a platform of making peace based on the "land for peace" formula – when he goes to Camp David, he puts on the table a far-reaching proposal, something that was not on the table before, certainly not directly with the Palestinians. His proposal addressed everything that we were told were the obstacles to peace and the things that the Palestinians wanted.

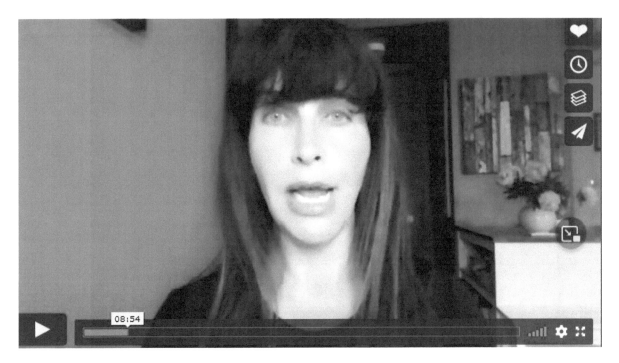

The occupation

We were told that the obstacle to peace is the occupation: Palestinians wanted to end the military presence of Israel in the West Bank and Gaza. On the table the proposal was that the Palestinians were going to have a **fully sovereign state**, an independent sovereign state in the West Bank and Gaza, thereby ending the occupation. Israeli was going to retreat, there was not going to be a military presence. So, ending the occupation was part of the proposal.

The settlements

What was the other obstacle we were told was the obstacle to peace? Settlements. So, the State of Palestine, the sovereign independent State of Palestine was going to have no settlements. Settlements were either to be removed and dismantled, or exchanged for equivalent land. So, the independent, sovereign State of Palestine was going to end the occupation and have no settlements. So, two obstacles removed.

Jerusalem

Then, what were we told? Jerusalem. Jerusalem was going to be divided: the Jewish neighborhoods to Israel, the Arab, secular, neighbors to Palestine and, then, the question of the Old City: the one square kilometer, which I fondly refer to it as "*the insanity center*", that one square kilometer was *also going to be divided*. Holy sites, we sometimes forget how far-reaching the proposal was, the Holy sites within the Old City were going to be divided between Israel and Palestine. So, if we were told that Jerusalem is the problem, an obstacle to peace, that was also taken care in the proposal. So, *check, check, check*.

All the Palestinians had to do was say "yes". And they would have had an end to the occupation, a sovereign state, no settlements, capital in East Jerusalem, including the Holy sites. They only had to say "yes". What do they do? They walk away. Arafat walks away.

OK. You might say walking away is a negotiating tactic. You know, that happens. Fair enough. But Arafat walks away – and by the way, eight years later, in 2008, Abu Mazen [Mahmoud Abbas], the heir of Arafat, walks away from a similar proposal by [Prime Minister] Ehud Olmert. Arafat walks away, and Abu Mazen later walks away, to no criticism from his own people. If this is the Palestinian aspiration you would expect, at least, someone to write an op-ed, a small NGO to be established, something, to say: *"Are you crazy? We could just have everything we wanted. Go back there into the negotiating room and get us our state"*. But there are no such voices. And I know that sometimes people say: *"Oh, you know, it is because you cannot criticize in this society, Palestinian society is not democratic."* Look at Russia today. People are holding signs, people are protesting, and the stakes there are much-much higher. Palestinian society has never been as oppressive as Russia, and yet, you see protests in Russia. You did not see protests against Arafat walking away among the Palestinians. Arafat, and later Abu Mazen, walk away. They walk away to no criticism from their own people. Meaning that, by walking away they *fulfill* what their people wanted.

And, what follows is bloody murder. What follows, especially after Arafat walks away, is a three-year campaign misnamed "the second Intifada", a campaign of butchery, massacre and terrorism. Some of you might remember the incinerated buses, entire families blown to bits for having a Seder [Passover celebration and meal] in a hotel, or from going to get pizza in Haifa. And this campaign, a butchery, is taking place in Israel's cities: in Tel-Aviv, in Haifa, in Be'er Sheva. Not in the settlements, you know, as they say: *"the problem is the settlements and the occupation in the West Bank"*. That is not where this campaign of butchery is taking place.

And a lot of Israelis, going through that – myself included – are asking a very simple question: *"**What do the Palestinians want?**"*

What do the Palestinians want?

What do they want? Because, clearly, a Palestinian State that ends the occupation, with no settlements and a capital in East Jerusalem, is not what they want. Or, you could say that they want that, but there is something that they want much, much more. There is something that they want so much more, that they are willing to walk away from all that – for that other thing. What is that other thing? And, what my co-writer [of our book] Adi Schwartz – a senior editor of the *Haaretz* [newspaper] – also a member of the Israeli Peace Camp, also believing in the "land for peace", and what myself realize, is that the answer was staring us in the face. Palestinians have told us all along what they wanted. We just did not listen. Or when we did listen, we kind of explained it away. We did not take it seriously. What did the Palestinians want more than a state, more than ending the occupation, more than no settlements, more than Jerusalem? They told us: "*From the river, from the Jordan River, to the Mediterranean Sea, Palestine will be free [of Jews]*". They have always claimed, as their absolute top priority, the establishment of an Arab Palestinian State *with no state for the Jewish people in any borders whatsoever*.

And that goal, which to the credit of the Palestinians, they have been pursuing consistently for over a century – that goal has not changed. And, unfortunately there has not been a moment where that goal has changed. The *means* of pursuing that goal have been different and in our book "*The war of return*", we focus on one of these means, the so called "Right of Return", which if you read the book is neither "right" nor "return", but merely a mechanism and an idea established by the Palestinians, following the war of 1948, in order to insure that the war never ends and that the idea of a sovereign Jewish state in even part of the land remains unacceptable and, hopefully in their view, something that you can undo. And this has been the goal.

An irreconcilable conflict

When Adi and I were doing our research for the book ["*The War of Return*"], we came across a remarkable analysis of the conflict by the British Foreign Minister after World War II, Ernest Bevin. If you know anything about Ernest Bevin – a friend to the Jewish people and to Zionism he was not. But Ernest Bevin, in explaining to the British Parliament in 1947 why Britain is reneging on the mandate that they received from the League of Nations to establish a Jewish State, basically giving back the mandate to the heir of the League of Nations, to the United Nations, he said the following: "*His Majesty, the government has come to the conclusion that the conflict in the land is irreconcilable*". He calls it irreconcilable. He goes on to detail, saying that there were two people in the land, Jews and Arabs. That there was no question that there are *two people*, two nations in the land. They are not religions. Jews and Arabs. Two distinct collectives. And he goes on to detail what the top priority is for each one of these collectives, for the Jews and for the Arabs. And he calls it a point of principle. And this is "*the top priority*". He says, for the Jews the point of principle, the top priority, is to establish a State. The Jews want a State. He says, for the Arabs the top priority, the point of principle, is to prevent the Jews from establishing a State in *any* part of the land. Notice how he defines the conflict. And this is the definition to the present day and has been the best predictor for the behavior of the two sides from 1947 to the present. He basically says: "*Look: the Jews want a State. Period. The Arabs want the Jews **not** to have a State*". Notice that he is not saying that the conflict is "the Jews want a State, the Arabs want a State, and they cannot agree on the borders and it is difficult to figure out how to divide the land". No. He really zeroes in in why the conflict is irreconcilable: because the Jews want a State and the Arabs want the Jews not to have a State. This is, by definition, something that is irreconcilable. Everything else you can divide. You can divide the land, you can divide the resources, you can have all kinds of economic and security arrangements. But the one thing that you cannot divide, the one difference that you cannot split is between the idea that the Jews want a State and the Arabs want the Jews not to have a State. It is simple as that. In that sense, the conflict is incredibly simple. Now, notice that what I have said right now does not in itself bare any judgement. It does not say that one side is good and the other side is bad and that this is a battle between good and evil. You can believe that the idea of a Jewish State in any borders is truly a horrific, unjustified idea.

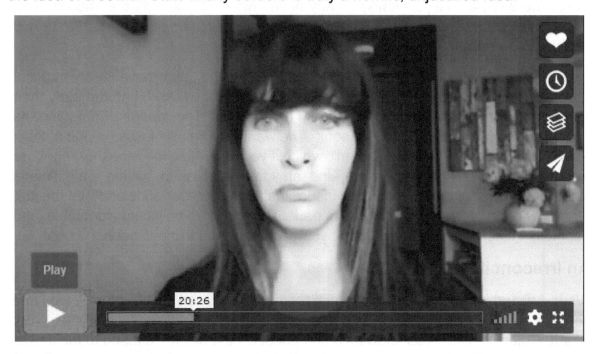

You can truly believe that the idea of a Jewish State in any border is in itself an injustice, which is generally the Palestinian world view. But that does not change the nature of the conflict. The nature of the conflict still remains the battle between those who want a Jewish State, generally the Jews, and, generally, the Arabs who want the Jews not to have a State. Regardless of whether you can think that the motivations of one side or the other are just or unjust, but this is the essence of the conflict. And this is why it is irreconcilable and this is why it has lasted for a century.

Now, how do we move from here? If this is the essence of the conflict, how does it end? And it actually ends in one of two ways. Quite simple. Either those who support a Jewish State will forgo their top priority, or those who believe that there should not be a Jewish State in any borders would forgo their top priority. That's it. That is how we get to a lasting peace. Either the Jews forgo their desire for a sovereign State, in essence, they say, "*you know, it is not worthy, there are other places to live, we are out of here*", or, the Arabs decide that they are willing to let a Jewish State exist, in

50

some borders. That is the only one of those two ways that the conflict ends. Truly resolved. Sometimes they say that the conflict is between Jewish Zionism and Arab anti-Zionism. For the conflict to end, either the Jews forgo their Zionism, the Jews forgo their desire for a sovereign State, or the Arabs forgo their anti-Zionism, Arabs forgo their belief that a Jewish State should not exist in any borders whatsoever. That's it. In the absence of one of these two outcomes the conflict continues. And in many ways, one can argue that the conflict has been a century-long battle of mutual exhaustion, where the Arabs are trying to exhaust the Jews into giving up on their aspirations for a State and for maintaining that State, and the Jews are trying to get the Arabs to forgo their aspiration for them not to be a Jewish State. That's it. And we have been engaged for more than a century in this battle of mutual exhaustion.

We are winning

And the reason that this has been going on for a century is that both sides see indications that they are winning: Jews look at their achievements, the establishment of their State, their various military victories, the prosperity of the State, the peace agreements, the Abraham Accords (and we will talk about them in a few minutes), and they say: The Arab world is finally coming to terms with the existence of the Jewish State. Hence, we can see the end of the conflict.

But the Arabs on the other side see it differently: No, the Jewish State is weak, Jews are arguing, young Jews abroad are renouncing Zionism, so we are seeing more and more Jews forgo their aspirations for a Jewish State. The world is calling the Jewish State an apartheid, the world is mobilizing in order to put an end to the Jewish State. So, we are winning.

And we only have to exhaust the other side.

So, this is where we are. This is what brings the conflict to an end. And, as I said, both sides believe that time is on their side. Just yesterday, someone tweeted "The Zionist experiment is not going to last for more than twenty years, it is showing its weaknesses, it is showing its contradictions. It is not going to last." And I have to say that, from their perspective, it is an entirely rational world view.

After we published the book, initially in Hebrew, Adi and I had many, many meetings with Western journalists and diplomats, especially those from countries who are funding UNWRA, the agency that constantly fuels the Palestinian world view that Israel is temporary. And we keep on telling them: "*Look, you think that you are funding some social services, but from the Palestinian perspective, every dollar that you are giving to UNWRA is a dollar Palestinians believe is a vote of support, on behalf of the West, to their belief that Israel is a temporary experiment destined to end in the near future*". And they say: "*Oh, that's not. The Palestinians know that it is a delusion, they understand that there is not going to be a return inside the sovereign State of Israel – which is what the Palestinians demand – so, you know, it is not going to happen. It is a delusion*". And we always tell them: Give the Palestinians the respect of believing and taking them at their word and that from their perspective and understanding of History, they are not delusional. They are opening a map, they see seven million Jews existing among half a billion Arabs, near one and a half billion Muslims, most of them continuing to be hostile to the idea of a Jewish State in any borders. And they, not irrationally, conclude that time is on their side. Which is why the traditional comparison of Palestinians is to "*colonizers*": We are like the French in Algeria, like the Crusaders – a state that lasted eighty-eight years, or more if you do not include Jerusalem. Recently they compared us to the Americans in Afghanistan. From their perspective, we are a foreign people, foreign colonizers who came to a land to which we had no connection, no historical affinity, no cultural connection. Stole the land, took it from people to whom it belonged and, therefore, like all foreigners, we – the Jews in Israel – are destined to leave, if we meet enough resistance and violence. This is the dominant narrative, not just among the Palestinians but in the Arab world. And, as I said, it is not delusional and it is not something plucked from thin air

What do we have on our side? Why, by and large, I am more optimistic these days than I have been for quite some time? Because I do see for the first time ever, the emergence of an alternative world view and narrative regarding Israel's position in the region.

The peace agreements that Israel made with Egypt and Jordan did not fundamentally alter the Arab narrative regarding Israel, that Israel is a foreign colonial, Western outpost in the region to which it has no connection and, therefore, will one day disappear. This is why the so-called peace agreements with Egypt and Jordan were really better understood as *non-aggression* pacts: there were barely any diplomatic relations, no tourism, no economic relations, no warmth. Egypt and Jordan continued to be promoters of anti-Israeli resolutions in the international bodies. Egypt remained the number one producer and promoter of anti-Semitic content in Arabic to the Arab-speaking world. And for decades Israelis were told that this is peace. This is what peace looks like in the Arab world. As long as the conflict with the Palestinians continue, this is the best that you can hope for.

The Abraham Accords

And then came the Abraham Accords with the Gulf states and later with Morocco: the UAE, Bahrain and Morocco. And those countries went all in. Immediate warm diplomatic relations, tourism, economic relations. My tweeter feed is full with every day news about a new agreement signed between Gulf countries and Morocco and Israel, in the fields of education, and space, and agriculture. They went all in. Within days of signing the Abraham Accords they changed their books, which tells you that you change your books *after* you sign the peace agreement, not before. And really everything is in one word: **Abraham**.

You could not think of a better word to flip the narrative. If the dominant narrative in the Arab world remains still that Israel is a foreign, colonial implant in the region, to which it has no connection and, therefore, is a temporary presence that will be ousted with enough resistance, patience and violence, then there is no better single word than to flip it by saying "**Abraham**".

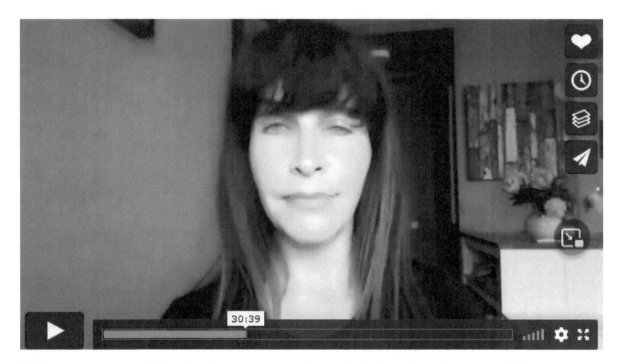

When you say *"Abraham"* you are acknowledging the Jews as kin, you are acknowledging the Jews as people with a history in the region, not as foreigners, but as people who belong, who have a deep, seeded, historical and cultural roots in the region. That their very identity as a people is wrapped up with the Land of Israel. And you can convey all of this by saying *"Abraham"*.

I am under no illusion that this has become the dominant narrative in the Arab world. I will say this: when this will become the dominant narrative in the Arab world – does not have to be exclusive – but when it becomes the dominant narrative – this will be the day that we will have peace. Everywhere. Because that is what the fundamental conflict is about. The fundamental conflict is not about – and has never been – about occupation or settlements, and not even about Jerusalem. It has always been about the Arab, and even broadly the Islamic world view, that a Jewish State in any borders in the region is an abomination, a gross injustice and something that, therefore, needs to be made to disappear, by any means: wars, terrorism, international condemnation, violence, "return". Whatever to get rid of this abomination which is the Jewish State. This is what the conflict is about. And for the first time ever in the history of the conflict we finally have a confident Arab and Muslim narrative that says the opposite.

After the Abraham Accords were signed, I became part of the Abraham Accords Group and I ended up with part of this group in almost a mirror image of what you hear among some young Jews in the West. They said: "We feel we have been lied to about Israel and Zionism and we want to understand". I ended up giving a lecture and talk about Zionism, to young Emiratis, Bahrainis, Moroccans. Following that, I published an op-ed with two young Emiratis, a man and a woman, that opens with the following line: "*We are a proud Muslim, a proud Arab, and we see no contradiction between that and also being Zionist.*" They actually said: "*We are Zionists*", they did not try to avoid that word. They said: "*We see no contradiction between the proud Muslim and Arab identity and between support for the right of the Jewish people to a sovereign State in at least part of their ancient homeland.*" So, for the first time we have a pro-Zionist, pro-Israel,

Arab position that recognizes Israel as a country that reflects an *indigenous people*, a people that have a deep historical and cultural connection to the land. And one of the most amazing developments, one that helps me make a very powerful point, is that as soon as the Gulf countries and Morocco became favorable towards Israel, they also became favorable towards Jews. And, you know, as a result of the ethnic cleansing of Jews from the Arab world, there are not many Jews in the Arab countries, but the UAE, Bahrain and Morocco are now going out of their way to show how much they want to celebrate Jewish life in their country. And they are not celebrating dead Jews. They are celebrating living Jews. My tweeter feed is full of Bahrainis and Emiratis, and Moroccans, holding celebrations of Jewish holidays with local Jews or Jewish ex-pats, and it helps me make the following point:

Anti-Zionism and Anti-Semitism

In the West today, quite a few are trying to claim that anti-Zionism is not against the Jews. You know, as long as the Jews are against Zionism, we love Jews and that anti-Zionism is just an ideology, about Israel. Now, I can split those hairs: anti-Zionism does not *always* necessarily have to be anti-Jewish. This is in theory. Except that *in practice* it always is. Every country, society, party, campus that have turned virulently anti-Zionist, in short order were hostile to Jewish life. So, when the Arab world made anti-Zionism a central tenet, within a short order it had no Jews. And those are Jews that pre-existed the Arab and Islamic conquest of the 7th century. The Soviet Union, as soon as it became anti-Zionist and made anti-Zionism a central tenet, it became a place that was hostile to Jews, and where Jews left as soon as they could. I could go on: Corbyn's Labor Party [in the UK], certainly American [universities] campuses.

When you make anti-Zionism a central tenet of who you are as a country, as a society, whatever the theory is – you are not a welcoming place for Jews.

And now, we are seeing the opposite: we are seeing that when Arab countries are embracing Israel, are embracing Zionism, understanding the historical connections between the Jewish people, the people of Israel and the Land of Israel, they also become welcoming and warm places for Jewish life. This is a very instructive example of the very deep connection between being warm towards Israel and Zionism and welcoming and being warm towards a prosperous Jewish life.

Conclusion

As I said, we are still stuck in the middle of this conflict. Fundamentally, it is a very simple conflict between Jewish Zionism and Arab anti-Zionism. Obviously, I would like this conflict to end not by Jews forgoing their State, but the Arabs forgoing their mobilization against the Jewish State. When that happens, I believe it will be the simplest negotiation. We will have a Jewish State living next to an Arab Palestinian State, but not before much of the Arab world – certainly the Palestinians – forgo the notion that having a Jewish State in any borders is some kind of abomination to which they must dedicate their lives to erase. And I will say this: in order to bring about that eventuality, sooner rather than later, we must make it clear to Palestinians and to the

Arab world at large that if their goal is "*from the River to the Sea*", if their goal is no Jewish State in any borders whatsoever, they will not have our sympathy and support. Not that of the West. But, if they finally adopt a path of having an Arab Palestinian State *next* to Israel, rather than instead of Israel, they will find everyone rushing to support them in that constructive cause.

So, thank you, and I will be very happy to discuss any ideas and questions.

Further reading*:*

The following book is recommended:

Adi Schwartz and Einat Wilf, "*The war of return: How western indulgence of the Palestinian dream has obstructed the path to peace*" (2020 edition)

A few added notes by the editor:

Palestinian refugees

"*Return of refugees*" is not an absolute right. There were many wars in the 20th century in Europe and Asia, with millions and millions of refugees. The policy adopted by the world in general and the United Nations in particular was *the resettlement of refugees in their new countries: for many reasons this policy was the humane thing to do*. The alternative was to encourage false illusions, instead of rebuilding their lives, and recurrent wars "*to settle accounts*". This policy made even more sense in the Palestinian case, since many of the original Palestinian refugees as a result of the 1948 war were not refugees but *internally displaced* persons: most of the refugees at the end of the 1948 war found themselves in refugee camps in the West Bank and Gaza, the land allocated to the Palestinian State. No one complained about the Arab states' occupation of the West Bank (by Jordan) and Gaza (by Egypt) from 1948 to 1967.

The Palestinian refugees became an exceptional case compared to the policies adopted regarding refugees in other wars in the world, due to the pressure exerted by the Arab states that did not want to accept the existence of an independent Jewish state in their midst. Their demand to the return of the original 700,000 Palestinian refugees from the 1948 war and their descendants – amounting today to several million Palestinians – to within the Israeli pre-1967 armistice borders was de-facto a continuation of the war with Israel by other means (the "war of return") with the same desired effect: the eradication of the Jewish State by eliminating the Jewish majority, returning the Jews to their previous status as a "*tolerated*" minority in Arab lands ("*dhimmis*") at best or their physical liquidation or expulsion at worst. This is the end result, irrespective of whether one drapes it in the language of the centuries-old reactionary religious Islam doctrine about the status of the Jews in Arab-conquered lands ("*dhimmis*") or in the new terminology of the "progressive" international Left, which defines Israel as "*a settler colonial project*".

Jewish refugees

At the beginning of the twentieth century almost one million Jews lived in the Arab countries, from North Africa to the Middle East. Hundreds of thousands of Jews had been living there for more than two thousand years, well before the 7th century Arab conquest of these lands. Many others dated from the time of the expulsion of the Jews from Spain and Portugal in the 15th century or before.

The dislocation of the Jewish refugees from Arab countries was total: in less than one generation-time 870,000 Jews were ethnically cleansed from the Arab countries, their properties confiscated and converted into refugees. The majority of these Jewish refugees – 608,799 refugees total – were absorbed by Israel: 129,539 from Iraq, 35,802 from Libya, 266,304 from Morocco, 8,523 from Syria, 52,518 from Tunisia, 50,619 from Yemen, 37,395 from Egypt, 24,067 from Algeria, 4,032 from Lebanon

Is the humiliation, loss, death, dispossession and ethnic cleansing suffered by 870,000 Jews in the Arab countries less valid?

Furthermore: *The Palestinian refugees were a result of being in a war zone and in the middle of armed hostilities. Violence against the Jews, their killing and displacement was also part and parcel of this war.* For example, during the initial stages of the war, in April 1948, a convoy of nurses, doctors and medical students set out for the Hebrew University, located on Mount Scopus, Jerusalem. They were assaulted by Arab militia: 75 Jews perished in the attack. In May 1948, four kibbutzim in Gush Etzion, next to Jerusalem, were completely destroyed and about 130 Jews – who had surrendered – were summarily executed, women and men.

On the other hand, *the Jewish refugees from the Arab countries were civilians far away from an armed conflict*, who were violently dispossessed and ethnically cleansed from vast lands extending from North Africa to the Middle East, just for being a defenseless and vulnerable minority in the midst of a Muslim majority led and inspired by a reactionary medieval Islamic doctrine about "*dhimmi*" people.

In recent years, it is gaining recognition among the international community that a lasting peace between Israel and the Arab countries will have to include a just resolution of the claims of the Jewish refugees from the Arab countries. [1]

Reference

[1] Martin Gilbert: "*In Ishmael house: A history of Jews in Muslim lands*" (2010, edition). See chapter 21, "*The search for recognition*", pages 325-334

Appendix 3.1: The Clinton parameters

In June 1967 a war between the Arab countries and Israel was triggered by the sudden blockade imposed by Egypt to Israel's maritime navigation through the straits of Tiran, in an intent to cut the economic ties between Israel and Asia. The war pitted Egypt, Syria and Jordan against Israel, and its effects are felt till today. The main results of this war were: Egypt lost the Sinai Peninsula and the Gaza Strip, Syria lost the Golan Heights, and Jordan lost the West Bank.

In November 1967 the United Nations Security Council adopted the resolution 242 that set the principles for the resolution of the conflict between Israel and the Arab countries.

The implementation of the 242 got a good start with the Egypt-Israel peace treaty signed in 1979. The next step was expected to be a peace treaty with Jordan. However, in a surprise move, Israel and the Palestine Liberation Organization (PLO) signed in 1993 the Oslo Accords, bypassing Jordan, who lost the West Bank to the PLO. This approach (nowadays called *"the 2-state solution"*) enjoyed a short-lived Golden Age in the late nineties: three Nobel Peace prizes were awarded. However, it soon hit its first reality check when in 2000 the PLO rejected the peace proposal presented by President Clinton, known as *"the Clinton parameters"*. Since then, this approach took a steep downturn from which it never recovered.

In his autobiographic book, *"My Life"*, published in 2005, President Clinton described the last weeks of the failed attempt to reach an accord between Israel and the PLO:

December 23 [2000, a few weeks before leaving office], was a fateful day for the Middle East peace process. After the two sides [Israelis and Palestinians] had been negotiating again for several days at Bolling Air Force Base [in Washington, DC], my team and I became convinced that unless we narrowed the range of debate, in effect forcing the big compromises up front, there would never be an agreement. Arafat [the Chairman of the PLO] was afraid of being criticized by other Arab leaders; Barak [Israel's Prime Minister] was losing ground [in the polls] to [the opposition leader] Sharon at home [a few weeks before the coming elections in Israel]. So I brought the Palestinian and Israeli teams into the Cabinet Room and read them my "parameters" for proceeding. These were developed after extensive private talks with the parties separately since Camp David [meetings held in July 2000]. If they accepted the parameters within four days, we would go forward. If not, we were through.

I read them slowly so that both sides could take careful notes. On territory, I recommended 94 to 96 percent of the West Bank for the Palestinians with a land swap from Israel of 1 to 3 percent, and an understanding that the land kept by Israel would include 80 percent of the settlers in blocs. On security, I said Israeli forces should withdraw over a three-year period while an international force would be gradually introduced, with the understanding that a small Israeli presence in the Jordan Valley could remain for another three years under the authority of the international forces. The Israelis would also be able to maintain their early-warning station in the West Bank with a Palestinian liaison presence. In the event of an "imminent and demonstrable threat to Israel's security," there would be provision for emergency deployments in the West Bank.

The new state of Palestine would be "nonmilitarized," but would have a strong security force; sovereignty over its airspace, with special arrangements to meet Israeli training and operational needs; and an international force for border security and deterrence.

On Jerusalem, I recommended that the Arab neighborhoods be in Palestine and the Jewish neighborhoods in Israel, and that the Palestinians should have sovereignty over the Temple Mount/Haram and the Israelis sovereignty over the Western Wall and the "holy space" of which it is a part, with no excavation around the wall or under the Mount, at least without mutual consent.

On refugees, I said that the new state of Palestine should be the homeland for refugees displaced in the 1948 war and afterward, without ruling out the possibility that Israel would accept some to the refugees according to its own laws and sovereign decisions, giving priority to the refugee populations in Lebanon. I recommended an international effort to compensate refugees and assist them in finding houses in the new state of Palestine, in the land-swap areas to be transferred to Palestine, in their current host countries, in other willing nations, or in Israel. Both parties should agree that this solution would satisfy United Nations Security Council Resolution 194.

Finally, the agreement had to clearly mark the end of the conflict and put an end to all violence. I suggested a new UN Security Council resolution saying that this agreement, along with the final release of Palestinian prisoners, would fulfill the requirements of resolutions 242 and 338.

I said these parameters were nonnegotiable and were the best I could do, and I wanted the parties to negotiate a final status agreement within them. After I left, Dennis Ross and other members of our team stayed behind to clarify any misunderstanding, but they refused to hear complaints. I knew the plan was tough for both parties, but it was time – past time – to put up or shut up. The Palestinians would give up the absolute right of return; they had always known they would have to, but they never wanted to admit it. The Israelis would give up East Jerusalem and parts of the Old City, but their religious and cultural sites would be preserved; it had been evident for some time that for peace to come, they would have to do that. The Israelis would also give up a little more of the West Bank and probably a larger land swap than Barak's last best offer, but they would keep enough to hold at least 80 percent of the settlers. And they would get a formal end to the conflict. It was a hard deal, but if they wanted peace, I thought it was fair to both sides

Arafat immediately began to equivocate, asking for "clarifications." But the parameters were clear; either he would negotiate within them or not. As always, he was playing for more time. I called Mubarak [the Egyptian president] and read him the points. He said they were historic and he could encourage Arafat to accept them.

On the twenty-seventh, Barak's [Israeli] cabinet endorsed the parameters with reservations, but all their reservations were within the parameters, and therefore subject to negotiations anyway. It was historic: an Israeli government had said that to get peace, there would be a Palestinian state in roughly 97% of the West Bank, counting the swap, and all of Gaza, where Israel also had settlements. The ball was in Arafat's court.

I was calling other Arab leaders daily to urge them to pressure Arafat to say yes. They were all impressed with Israel's acceptance and told me they believed Arafat should take the deal. I have no way of knowing what they told him, though the Saudi ambassador, Prince Bandar, later told me he and Crown Prince Abdullah [of Saudi Arabia] had the distinct impression Arafat was going to accept the parameters.

On the twenty-ninth, Dennis Ross met with Abu Ala [a leading member of the Palestinian delegation], whom we all respected, to make sure Arafat understood the consequences of rejection. I would be gone. Ross would be gone. Barak would lose the upcoming election to Sharon. Bush wouldn't want to jump in after I had invested so much and failed.

I still didn't believe Arafat would make such a colossal mistake.

...

We passed up Renaissance Weekend again that year so that our family could spend the last New Year's at Camp David. I still hadn't heard from Arafat. On New Year's Day, I invited him to the White House the next day. Before he came, he received Prince Bandar and the Egyptian ambassador at his hotel. One of Arafat's younger aides told us that they had pushed him hard to say yes. When Arafat came to see me, he asked a lot of questions about my proposal. He wanted Israel to have the Wailing Wall, because of its religious significance, but asserted that the remaining fifty feet of the Western Wall should go to the Palestinians. I told him he was wrong, that Israel should have the entire wall to protect itself from someone using one entrance of the tunnel that ran beneath the wall from damaging the remains of the temples beneath the Haram. The Old City has four quarters: Jewish, Muslim Christian, and Armenian. It was assumed that Palestine would get the Muslim and Christian quarters, with Israel getting the other two. Arafat argued that he should have a few blocks of the Armenian quarter because of the Christian churches there. I couldn't believe he was talking to me about this.

Arafat was also trying to wiggle out of giving up the right of return. He knew he had to but was afraid of the criticism he would get. I reminded him that Israel had promised to take some of the refugees from Lebanon whose families had lived in what was now northern Israel for hundreds of years, but that no Israeli leader would ever let in so many Palestinians that the Jewish character of the state could be threatened in a few decades by the higher Palestinian birthrate. There were not going to be two majority-Arab states in the Holy Land; Arafat had acknowledged that by signing the 1993 peace agreement with its implicit two-state solution. Besides, the agreement had to be approved by Israeli citizens in a referendum. The right of return was a deal breaker. I wouldn't think of asking the Israelis to vote for it. On the other hand, I thought the Israelis would vote for a final settlement within the parameters I had laid out. If there was an agreement, I even thought Barak might be able to come back and win the election, though he was running well behind Sharon in the polls, in an electorate frightened by the intifada and angered by Arafat's refusal to make peace.

At times Arafat seemed confused, not wholly in command of the facts. I had felt for some time that he might not be at the top of his game any longer, after all the years of spending the night in different places to dodge assassins' bullets, all the countless hours on airplanes, all the endless hours of tension-filled talks. Perhaps he simply couldn't make the final jump from revolutionary to statesman. He had grown used to flying from place to place, giving mother-of-pearl gifts made by Palestinian craftsmen to world leaders and appearing on television with them. It would be different if the end of violence took Palestine out of the headlines and instead he had to worry about providing jobs, schools, and basic services. Most of the young people on Arafat's team wanted him to take the deal. I believe Abu Ala and Abu Mazen also would have agreed but didn't want to be at odds with Arafat.

When he left, I still had no idea what Arafat was going to do. His body language said no, but the deal was so good I couldn't believe anyone would be foolish enough to let it go. Barak wanted me to come to the region, but I wanted Arafat to say yes to the Israelis on the big issues embodied in my parameters first. In December the parties had met at Bolling Air Force Base for talks that didn't succeed because Arafat wouldn't accept the parameters that were hard for him.

Finally, Arafat agreed to see Shimon Peres on the thirteenth [of January 2001] after Peres had first met with Saeb Erekat. Nothing came of it. As a backstop, the Israelis tried to produce a letter with as much agreement on the parameters as possible, on the assumption that Barak would lose the election and at least both sides would be bound to a course that could lead to an agreement. Arafat wouldn't even do that, because he didn't want to be seen conceding anything. The parties continued their talks in Taba, Egypt [at the end of January 2001, after Bill Clinton left office]. They got close, but did not succeed. Arafat never said no; he just couldn't bring himself to say yes. Pride goeth before the fall.

Right before I left office [on January 20, 2001], Arafat, in one of our last conversations, thanked me for all my efforts and told me what a great man I was. "Mr. Chairman," I replied, "I am not a great man. I am a failure, and you have made me one." I warned Arafat that he was single-handedly electing Sharon and that he would reap the whirlwind.

In February 2001, Ariel Sharon would be elected prime minister in a landslide. The Israelis had decided that if Arafat wouldn't take my offer he wouldn't take anything, and that if they had no partner for peace, it was better to be led by the most aggressive, intransigent leader available. Sharon would take a hard line toward Arafat and would be supported in doing so by Ehud Barak and the United States. Nearly a year after I left office, Arafat said he was ready to negotiate on the basis of the parameters I had presented. Apparently, Arafat had thought the time to decide, five minutes to midnight, had finally come. His watch had been broken a long time.

Arafat's rejection of my proposal after Barak accepted it was an error of historic proportions. However, many Palestinians and Israelis are still committed to peace. Someday peace will come, and when it does, the final agreement will look a lot like the proposals that came out of Camp David and the six long months that followed.

The Old City of Jerusalem

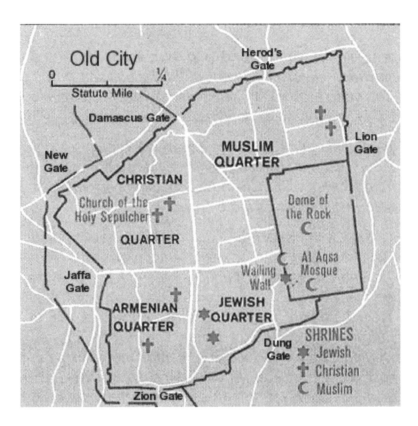

Map of the Old City of Jerusalem showing its four quarters (Muslim, Christian, Armenian and Jewish), as well as the location of the Muslim, Christian and Jewish shrines. The Old City occupies and area of about ¾ by ½ square miles, that is, 0.375 square miles (Photo from Wikipedia)

According to President Clinton's proposal, the Muslim and Christian quarters would be part of the Palestinian state, and the Armenian and Jewish quarters part of Israel. The Palestinians would have sovereignty over the Temple Mount/Haram (Dome of the Rock and Al Aqsa Mosque), and the Israelis would have sovereignty over the Western Wall (Wailing Wall). Any work or excavation around the wall or under the Mount would need the mutual consent of both parts.

The Israelis accepted President Clinton's proposal. The Palestinians did not.

Appendix 3.2

A different history of displacement and loss

By **Matti Friedman**

[Published in the newspaper *Times of Israel*, May 15, 2012]

"There is more than one way to look at the commemoration of 1948's Palestinian defeat and dispersion.

On May 15, many in the Arab world and elsewhere mark the Nakba, or the "Catastrophe", mourning the displacement of the Palestinian Arabs during the 1948 war with Israel. This year, as always, the commemoration will obscure the collapse at the same time of a different Arab society that few remember.

I have spent a great deal of time in the past four years interviewing people born and raised in Aleppo, Syria. Some of these people, most of whom are now in the eighties, are descended from families with roots in Aleppo going back more than two millennia, to Roman times. None of them lives there now.

On November 30, 1947, a day after the United Nations voted to partition Palestine into two states, one for Arabs and one for Jews, Aleppo erupted. Mobs stalked Jewish neighborhoods, looting houses and burning synagogues; one man I interviewed remembered fleeing his home, a barefoot nine-year-old, moments before it was set on fire. Abetted by the government, the rioters burned 50 Jewish shops, five schools, 18 synagogues and an unknown number of homes. The next day the Jewish community's wealthiest families fled, and in the following months the rest began sneaking out in small groups, most of them headed to the new state of Israel. They forfeited their property, and faced imprisonment or torture if they were caught. Some disappeared en route. But the risk seemed worthwhile: in Damascus, the capital, rioters killed 13 Jews, including eight children, in August 1948, and there were similar events in other Arab cities.

At the time of the UN vote, there were about 10,000 Jews in Aleppo. By the mid-1950s there were 2,000 living in fear of the security forces and the mob. By the early 1990s no more than a handful remained, and today there are none. Similar scripts played out across the Islamic world. Some 850,000 Jews were forced from their homes.

If we are to fully understand the Israel-Arab conflict, the memory of these people and their exodus must be acknowledged – not as a political weapon, a negotiating tactic or as part of a competition about who suffered more, but simply as history without which it is impossible to understand Israel and the way the Arab world sees it.

Everyone knows the Palestinian refugees are part of the equation of Mideast peace, and anyone who is interested can visit a Palestinian refugee camp and hear true and wrenching stories of expulsion and loss. Among the Jews expelled by Arabs, on the other hand, one can find few who think of themselves as refugees or define themselves by their dispossession. Most are citizens of Israel.

Of the 20 families in my fairly average Jerusalem apartment building, half are in Israel because of the Arab expulsion of Jews, and this is representative of Israel as a whole. According to the Israeli demographer Sergio Della Pergola of Hebrew University, though intermarriage over two or three generations has muddled the statistics, roughly half of the 6 million Jews in Israel today came from the Muslim world or are descended from people who did. Many Arabs, and many Israelis, consider Israel a Western enclave in the Middle East. But these numbers do not support that view.

These Jews have shaped Israel and are a key force in the country's political life. They also make Israel very different from the American Jewish community, which is overwhelmingly rooted in Europe. They are a pillar of Israel's right wing, particularly of the Likud party. They maintain a wary view of Israel's neighbors – a view that has been strengthened by the actions of the Palestinians but that is rooted in their own historical experience and in what might be considered an instinctive understanding of the region's unkind realities.

The legacy of their exodus in the countries they left behind is harder to detect, but it, too, is significant.

In many Arab towns and cities there is an area where Jews used to live. In some cities, like Cairo [Egypt], this area is still called 'harat al-yahud', the Jewish Quarter. Reporting there several years ago I found people who could show me the location of a certain abandoned synagogue, which they knew by name. A man who once showed me around Fez, Morocco, knew exactly where the old Jewish neighborhood, the 'mellah', had been, though there was not a single Jew there and had not been for many years. There are remnants like this in Aleppo [Syria], Tripoli [Lybia], Baghdad [Iraq] and elsewhere. The people who live in or around the Jews' old homes still know who used to own them and how they left; this extinct Jewish world might have been forgotten elsewhere, but millions in the Arab world see evidence of it every day.

As I have reported this nearly invisible story, it has occurred to me that we often hate most the things or people that remind us of something we dislike about ourselves, and that here lies one of the hidden dynamics of the Israel-Arab conflict. It is one papered over by the simple narrative of Nakba Day, which posits that a foreign implant displaced a native community in 1948 and that the Palestinian Arabs are paying the price for the European Holocaust. This narrative, chiefly designed to appeal to Western guilt, also conveniently erases the uncomfortable truth that half of Israel's Jews are there not because of the Nazis, but because of the Arabs themselves.

Israel is not as foreign to the Middle East as many of its neighbors like to pretend, and more than one native community was displaced in 1948. If many in the Arab world insist, as they do each Nakba Day, that Israel is a Western invader that must be repelled, it is a claim that belongs to the realm not only of politics but of psychology – one that helps repress their own knowledge that the country they try to portray as alien is also the vengeful ghost of the neighbors they wronged."

***

Matti Friedman is a journalist and author. Born in Toronto and based in Jerusalem, his work appears regularly in the *New York Times*, *The Atlantic* and *Tablet*.

Lesson 4

Context: Saturday and Sunday people

First the Saturday people

Suppose a man leaps out of a burning building – and lands on a bystander in the street below. The burning building is supposed to be Europe, the jumper is the Jew, and the unfortunate bystander the Palestinian Arab. This metaphor for the Arab-Israeli conflict was apparently coined by writer Isaac Deutscher and has been approvingly cited by the late polemicist and author Christopher Hitchens.

Whilst it is a striking image, this analogy is, of course, inherently problematic. It propagates the assumption that Jews came from Europe to displace innocent natives. Now try a different analogy. Imagine that the building is actually situated in the Middle East, a short distance from a homestead by the sea originally settled by the Jews. Some 3,000 years ago and until recent times, the Jew inhabited the main house alongside other indigenous residents in the Middle East. The homestead was seized by the Romans in 70 CE and most of its residents dispersed. An occupier arrived in the seventh century, and took over the whole region. In the twentieth century arsonists set fire to the main building, forcing the Jew to jump out of the window. "First the Saturday people, then the Sunday people" [1]: Armenians, Assyrians, Chaldean Christians, Maronites, Copts, also jumped for their lives. And not just the Sunday people: Mandaeans, Yazidis and 'heretical' and sectarian Muslims have been jumping out of the windows too. The difference is that the Jew found refuge in the embattled homestead, his original abode. Populating it continuously through 2,000 years, Jews never surrendered its title.

More than 99 per cent of Jewish residents have fled from the Arab world in the last sixty years. Some 650,000 went to Israel and 200,000 to the West. Their exodus took two forms: those better equipped with foreign passports and connections generally engineered their private exits, mainly to Europe, Australia, or the Americas. Together with a minority of ideological Zionists, the rest went to Israel. Although the diaspora remains overwhelmingly Ashkenazi, over 50 per cent of Israel's Jews today are Mizrahi or Sephardi refugees from Arab and Muslim countries or their descendants.

Mass refugee movements have been a feature of conflicts in the first half of the twentieth century: upwards of fifty-two million people have been displaced. The Arab-Israeli conflict is no exception. However, the root causes of the mass displacement of the Jews predate the Arab-Israeli conflict, and it may be argued that the inability of Arabs and Muslims to accept Israel belongs in deep-seated cultural, religious and ideological prejudice.

The twentieth century produced 135 million refugees as a consequence of the self-determination of peoples through violence. Population exchanges were common in the twentieth century – roughly equal numbers of Jews from the Middle East and North Africa, and Palestinian Arabs swapped places. There were also exchanges of refugees between Greece and Turkey, India and Pakistan, and Greek and Turkish Cyprus, not forgetting the mass migration of ethnic Germans and others in the wake of the Second World War.

However, while all these refugee populations have been absorbed in their new countries, only the Palestinian Arabs are still, according to the UN, considered refugees and allowed to pass on their refugee status to succeeding generations ad infinitum. Their leaders have constantly kindled the vain hope of a 'Right of Return' to Palestine in their hearts, even though most were not born there and some had been resident for no more than two years [2]. Arguably, these refugees have been deliberately deprived of civil rights in their adopted countries in order to remain a standing reproach to Israel and a weapon in the decades-long Arab and Muslim struggle against the Jewish state.

***

The above is an excerpt from the Preface of the book "***Uprooted: How 3,000 years of Jewish civilization in the Arab world vanished overnight***", by Lyn Julius

Lyn Julius is the daughter of Iraqi-Jewish refugees who fled Iraq in 1950.

Notes

[1] See next section: "**Religious intolerance or national oppression?**"

[2] Lyn Julius refers here to the 2-year residence clause to qualify as Palestinian refugee: it was explicitly added so that a certain number of people displaced by the Arab-Israeli 1948 war could qualify as being Palestinian refugees, even if they had not resided in Palestine for long. The UNHCR protocols refer to "refugees" as "persons that left their habitual residence under duress", usually war. The concept of having been an "habitual resident" in his/her country of origin is used repeatedly as a qualification for refugee status, with "habitual residence" being defined as "*the place where a person resided on an ongoing and stable basis.*" The added "2-year residence" re-defined, or clarified, the meaning of the condition "habitual residence" for Palestinian refugees.

Putting this in historical context: the Jews were not the only people who begun repopulating Palestine at the beginning of the 20th century. There was also an influx of other people, seasonal laborers and skilled workers, pouring from neighboring Arab countries, as a result of the increased economic activity in Palestine brought by the Jews. The "2-year" clause was meant to include these other newcomers, who – with the break of hostilities between Israel and the neighboring Arab countries in 1948 – many of them were relabeled as "Palestinian refugees".

Religious intolerance or national oppression?

"An occupier arrived in the seventh century, and took over the whole region. In the twentieth century arsonists set fire to the main building, forcing the Jew [in the Arab countries] to jump out of the window. "First the Saturday people, then the Sunday people": Armenians, Assyrians, Chaldean Christians, Maronites, Copts, also jumped for their lives. And not just the Sunday people: Mandaeans, Yazidis and 'heretical' and sectarian Muslims have been jumping out of the windows too. The difference is that the Jew found refuge in the embattled homestead, his original abode. Populating it continuously through 2,000 years, Jews never surrendered its title."

Lyn Julius, ""Uprooted: How 3,000 years of Jewish civilization in the Arab world vanished overnight"

Joel Veldkamp, a director of the *"Christian Solidarity International"* organization, had an interesting observation [1]: at first sight one could interpret that we are dealing here with a problem of *religious intolerance in the Islamic world*. This is not the case. According to Veldkamp, referring to the Armenian genocide in 1915:

*"Today, we have become used to thinking of religious persecution as, by definition, an attack on religious freedom. Yet the twentieth century's worst instance of anti-Christian persecution – the Armenian genocide – did not fit the "religious freedom" category so neatly. The architects of the genocide were not, after all, trying to keep Armenians from worshipping Jesus, building churches, or reading the Bible … They were trying to exterminate a Christian **people** (whether practicing or not) that they had long held in subservience but had come to see as a threat to their power."*

The second example provided by Lyn Julius, the *Assyrians*, is perfectly clear, especially for Jews. The Jews know who the Assyrians are: *they are not a religious community*. In the peak of their hegemony, the Assyrians forcefully exiled the Jews to Mesopotamia in 721 BC, after they conquered the kingdom of Israel, marking the historical beginning of the Jewish diaspora. The Assyrians are an ancient *people,* not a religious community. Assyrians speak a native language commonly known as Assyrian, neo-Aramaic, or Syriac. It is a pre-Arabic language that derives directly from Aramaic, the ancient lingua franca of the Middle East. Assyrians are overwhelmingly Christian: They were the first *people* that adopted Christianity (in the first century CE.), well before the Christian religion was adopted in Europe. As in the case of the Jews and the Armenians, the Assyrians became another non-Muslim minority in the lands conquered by the Muslim expansion after the 7th century. The Assyrians suffered their own genocide during World War I in the hands of the Muslim Ottoman Empire: around 275,000 Assyrians were killed in 1915. Another massacre of the Assyrian people occurred later in Iraq, in August 1933, when over 100 Assyrian villages were destroyed and looted, and an estimated several thousand Assyrians were killed. The accounts of this latter massacre were horrific. One was given by the Patriarch of the Assyrian Church, Mar Eshai Shimun XXIII (published close to the events, on February 1934) [2]:

"The inoffensive population was indiscriminately massacred, men, women and children alike, with rifle, revolver, and machine gun fire … Priests were tortured and their bodies mutilated. Those who showed their Iraqi nationality papers were the first to be shot. Girls were raped and women violated and made to march naked before the Arab army commander. Holy books were used as fuel for burning girls. Children were run over by military cars. Pregnant women were bayoneted. Children were flung in the air and pierced on to the points of bayonets. Those who survived in the other villages were now exposed day and night to constant raids and acts of violence. Forced conversion to Islam of men and women was the next process. Refusal was met with death."

The Assyrian people are today dispersed over the whole world. Their total number is around 3-5 million. Their largest communities are in Iraq, Syria, the United States, Sweden and Germany.

The massacre of the Assyrian minority in Iraq, in August 1933, occurred only a few months after Iraq had obtained independence. The implications for the then Jewish minority in Palestine had the Jewish leaders worried [2]. Eight years later, in 1941, over 180 Jews were murdered in a pogrom in Baghdad. Then, in 1948, Iraq participated in the invasion of the Arab armies in their intent to eliminate the nascent Jewish State.

The Muslim colonizers

From Mecca in the Arabian Peninsula, and from the 7th century on, Muslims began an expansion and conquest of vast territories, extending from the Middle East in the north, to North Africa in the west. Many minorities became suddenly entrapped and embedded in the new Muslim-dominated world. Some of these minorities disappeared over time, following a process of forced Islamization. Others put a high value on their history, and kept on for centuries their cultural traditions, language, and religion, in spite of the pressure and oppression of their Muslim colonizers.

In the next section, we will go back to the Jews, who suffered the successive colonization of the Greeks, the Romans, and the Arabs.

References

[1] Joel Veldkamp, *"The persecution of Armenian Christians is not just a religious freedom issue",* October 3, 2023

https://www.firstthings.com/web-exclusives/2023/10/the-persecution-of-armenian-christians-is-not-just-a-religious-freedom-issue

[2] Paul A. Isaac, *"The Urgent Reawakening of the Assyrian Question in an Emerging Iraqi Federalism: The Self-Determination of the Assyrian People",* Northern. Illinois University Law Review 209 (2008)

https://huskiecommons.lib.niu.edu/niulr/vol29/iss1/4/

Palestine and the Jewish Diaspora

The Jews occupied a *unique geographic position* in the Middle East: they lived in a strategic place, the transit point between three continents, a coveted place for all the large imperial powers of the time. They had a *unique philosophy*: the Jews worshiped one and only one God, declared this God to be invisible and, on top of it, proclaimed that there were no other gods. This only brought on them the ire of all the imperial powers of the time, like the Greeks and the Romans, who worshiped a variety of multiple idols. And they had a *unique history*: "*Remember that we were slaves in Egypt*", parents told to their children during the Passover meal, from time immemorial. This is central to the Jewish ethos. What other people would include in their primordial mythos that they descended from slaves? This did not sit well with the great powers of that era, for which slavery was a very profitable endeavor, vital for their economy. All this – unique geographic position, unique philosophy, and unique history – put the Jews at odds with their surroundings. The result was that they lost their territorial center through frequent wars and became dispersed. Most historians set the origin of this dispersion (the Jewish Diaspora) in the years 66-73 CE, during the Jewish revolt against the Roman Empire, that ended with the destruction of Jerusalem. However, the true catastrophic event for the Jewish people was their last revolt against the Roman Empire, in years 132-136 CE, known as the *Bar Kokhba Revolt*, for the name of their leader. In this last rebellion, 985 villages in Judea were destroyed and around 580,000 Jews perished. [1]

Figure 4.1: Judea under Bar Kochba rule (132-136 CE)

After the Jewish rebellion in Judea was crushed, the Romans barred the remaining Jews from living in Jerusalem, and merged the Roman provinces of Syria and Judea, under one unified province, renamed "Syria Palaestina". The name "Palaestina" refers to an ancient people, the biblical "Philistines", who used to dwell in times past at the coast of the Mediterranean Sea, and were often at odds with the Jews. Having just eliminated the Jews of Judea physically, it seems that the Romans decided to eliminate also the name Judea from the maps. However, since then, the name "Palestine" stuck in all the Western literature as the land (or former land) of the Jews.

After the destruction of Judea in the 2nd century CE, the center of Jewish life in Palestine moved from the mountainous region of Judea to the Galilee, what is now northern Israel. In the course of several centuries the Jews in Galilee created two monumental works that shaped for centuries the life of the Jews in the Diaspora: the **Jerusalem Talmud** and the **Aleppo Codex**.

The "*Jerusalem Talmud*" was originally written by rabbinic sages in Tiberias, a town by the Sea of Galilee, *in the 4th century* (a century later, a second version of the *Talmud,* known as the *"Babylonian Talmud"*, was written by the Jewish center in Babylon, today Iraq). The importance of the Talmud cannot be understated: with the Jewish State gone and Jews living under foreign occupation in Palestine, or in foreign lands in the diaspora, the rabbinic sages pondered the question of how to preserve Jewish life in such conditions. The answer was the Talmud: an encyclopedic compilation of myriads of examples and teachings covering all the subjects of Jewish life, from Jewish customs, to religious and civil affairs. The Talmud became for centuries the main source of Jewish survival *in the Diaspora*: Jews in the Diaspora followed the Talmud for guidance in everything related to earthly and spiritual affairs.

Figure 4.2 shows a page of the "*Jerusalem Talmud*" found in the *geniza* of the Ben Ezrah synagogue in Fustat, Egypt. (Remember the name "*Fustat*": we will find it again when talking about the "Aleppo Codex").

Figure 4.2: A page of the "*Jerusalem Talmud*", found in the "geniza" (storage room) of Ben Ezra Synagogue in Fustat, Egypt.

The Aleppo Codex – a special text of the Bible– ***was written in Tiberias around 930 CE***. It became the most authoritative version of the Hebrew Bible, followed by the Jews in the Diaspora.

Written Hebrew only uses the consonants: vowels are not printed. If you check the archeological remains of ancient Hebrew texts written two thousand years ago in the Land of Israel, you will not find vowels in these texts. No one needed them, because Jews lived then in Israel, Hebrew was quite natural to them, and it was clear to all how to read and pronounce the words in the sacred texts, even if no vowels were indicated in them. If you check the Sacred Scrolls of the Bible today in any synagogue over the world, there are no vowels either written in the text. So how come, Jews so far apart in time and space, today in New York, in Buenos Aires, in London, in Moscow and in Jerusalem, preserved for 2,000 years the phonetics of the Hebrew language and manage to read and pronounce the words in the Bible with such uniformity during the long centuries of dispersion in the Diaspora?

The answer can be found in **Tiberias**, the city at the shores of the Sea of Galilea. The Jewish sages in Tiberias came to the help of their brethren in the Diaspora: they meticulously added the vowels to all the words in a copy of the Bible, and not only vowels but also diacritical marks so people would know how to pronounce each word with the correct stressed syllable, and thus, the **Aleppo Codex** was born.

Figures 4.3 and 4.4 show the difference between a standard Bible text you can find today in a synagogue and the biblical text as it appears in the "Aleppo Codex":

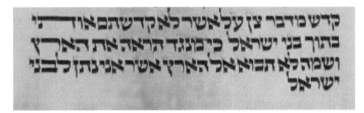

Figure 4.3: text in a standard scroll of the Bible. For example, the last word in the text (fourth row, to the right) is the word "*Israel*" in Hebrew. Notice the absence of vowels, or any marks above and below the word "*Israel*" or any other word in the text.

Figure 4.4: To the right is shown a paragraph of the Aleppo Codex. To the left, the word "*Israel*" that appears in the paragraph is reproduced and magnified. The vowels in the word "*Israel*" were added below the letters. In addition to the vowels, the Aleppo Codex includes diacritical marks for the correct pronunciation of the words.

The Aleppo Codex circulated between the Jewish communities in the Middle East (see Figure 4.5 and accompanying text, and reference [2].) The movement from Tiberias to Jerusalem in year 1030, may be related to a major earthquake along the Jordan Valley, in 1033, which might have damaged Tiberias. The movement from Jerusalem to Egypt was related to historic events in the region: The book had been caught by the Christian Crusaders, during their military expeditions in 1095-1291, and was redeemed by the Jewish community in Egypt by paying a ransom. Fustat, the city in Egypt where the Aleppo Codex was moved to after it was retrieved from the Crusaders, had an important Jewish community: The Jewish philosopher and physician Maimonides (1138-1204) lived in Fustat.

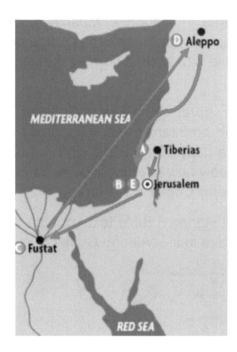

930 : written in Tiberias
1030 : moved to Jerusalem
1100 : moved to Egypt
1375: moved to Aleppo
1947: disappeared during the pogrom
        and burning of the Great Synagogue
1957: appeared in Jerusalem
1958-2023: The Israel Museum, Jerusalem

Figure 4.5: The travel history of the Aleppo Codex (early dates are approximate)

The book was later moved from Fustat to Aleppo, in Syria, in year 1375. The movement of the "Aleppo Codex" from Fustat to Aleppo, may be related to the deterioration of the conditions of Jews (and Christians Copts) in Egypt during the rule of the Mamelukes. It is known that severe persecution and attacks against non-Muslims happened in 1354, close to the date when the "Aleppo Codex" was moved out of Egypt.

The Jewish community in Aleppo had the book for almost 600 years (hence, its name "Aleppo Codex"), until the pogrom in 1947, when the synagogue where it was kept was burnt. During the exodus of the Jews from Syria, following the pogroms in Aleppo (1947) and Damascus (1949), the book disappeared and, somehow, found its way to the recently born state of Israel, and it is now kept in the Israel Museum, Jerusalem.

Figure 4.6: The "Aleppo Codex", presently kept in the Israel Museum, Jerusalem

References

[1] These numerical figures were provided by the Roman historian Cassius Dio (born 150, died 235 CE), in his *History of Rome*, 69.14.1-2, cited in:

https://en.wikipedia.org/wiki/Bar_Kokhba_revolt

[2] Travelogue of the Aleppo Codex

https://www.biblicalarchaeology.org/daily/biblical-topics/hebrew-bible/travelogue-of-the-aleppo-codex/

Lexicon:

"*Geniza*": storage area in a Jewish synagogue designated for the storage of worn-out Hebrew-language books and papers on religious topics, prior to proper cemetery burial.

The "*Cairo Geniza*" is a collection of some 400,000 Jewish manuscript fragments that were kept in the geniza of the Ben Ezra Synagogue in Fustat, Egypt. These manuscripts span the entire period of Middle-Eastern, North African, and Spanish Jewish history between the 6th and 19th centuries CE, and comprise the largest and most diverse collection of medieval manuscripts in the world.

Appendix 4.1: Herodotus on Palestine

Herodotus (484-425 BC), a Greek historian and geographer, mentions the name "Palestine" several times in his book "*History*", usually in conjunction with Syria:

"Thence they went on to invade Egypt, and when they were in Syria which is called Palestine, Psammetichos king of Egypt met them; and by gifts and entreaties he turned them from their purpose: and as they retreated, when they came to the city of Ascalon in Syria, …

(Note: "*Ascalon*", also known as "*Ashkelon*", a city in southern Israel, at the coast of the Mediterranean Sea. Ashkelon is known in the Bible as the place where Delilah, a lady from Philistine, cut Samson's hair, draining thus the source of his strength)

However, in another place Herodotus is more specific, differentiating Palestine from Syria, and identifying Palestine along the coast of the Mediterranean, and in the path between Syria and Egypt:

"These Phoenicians dwelt in ancient time, as they themselves report, upon the Erythraian Sea, and thence they passed over and dwell in the country along the sea coast of Syria; and this part of Syria and all as far as Egypt is called Palestine."

(Note: The "*Erythraian Sea*" is known today as the "*Red Sea*")

This places "Palestine" at the coast of the Mediterranean Sea, in the biblical place where the "Philistines" lived (and the Philistines, as Phoenicians left behind in the southern strip by the Mediterranean Sea, in their wandering from the Red Sea to Lebanon, where they finally settled):

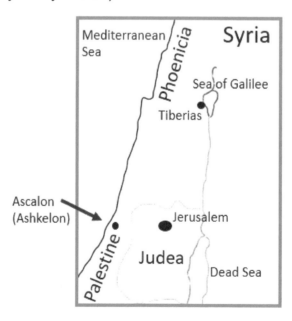

Reference

Herodotus, "*History*", translated from Greek by G. C. Macaulay (New York, 1890)

https://archive.org/details/HerodotusHistory

Lesson 5

A Brief History of the Jews: Sephardi, Mizrahi and Ashkenazi Jews

How to compress 3,500 years of *"History of the Jewish People"* in a few pages, for students in a compulsory *"Ethnic Studies"* course in California's K12 schools?

First things first: do not let an ignorant, posing as an *"educator"*, confuse you: Jews are not divided between the *"oppressed"* American Jews of Sephardi or Middle Eastern origin (whose status in California schools is being upgraded lately to *"Jews of color"*) and the *"white"* *"oppressing"* American Jews of Ashkenazi or European origin.

Who are the Sephardi Jews?

Historically, the Sephardi Jews were for centuries the "aristocracy" of the Jewish people in the Diaspora, due both to their higher cultural as well as economic status. The first Jews that settled in America were Sephardi Jews, back in year 1654. They settled in New Amsterdam, what is today part of Manhattan, New York.

I happen to read fluently Ladino, the daily language of the Sephardi Jews: the *classic* Spanish Literature course I took in High-School in Buenos Aires, included reading original works by Spanish writers and poets from the 14th and 15th centuries. Theirs *was* the daily language spoken by the Jews in Spain, before they were expulsed in 1492, creating the Sephardi Diaspora (*"Sepharad"* is the Hebrew name for *"Spain"*). A few years later, in 1496, Jews were expelled from the adjacent Portugal. *Jews whose origin can be traced back to Spain and Portugal are called collectively the Sephardi Jews.* The Ladino Jewish songs and melodies are beautiful and share the sensuality of the old Spanish culture.

Sephardi Jews had also their great scholars, like Maimonides and Spinoza. Maimonides was a physician and philosopher. He was born in 1138 in Cordoba, Spain, which at that time was under Muslim rule. He evaded forced conversion to the Islam by fleeing to Egypt, where he served as personal physician of Saladin, the first sultan of Egypt. His most notable philosophical writing was *"The Guide for the Perplexed"*, written in Arabic using the Hebrew alphabet. Baruch Spinoza, born in Amsterdam, Holland, in 1632, came from a family of Portuguese Jews that fled the Spanish Inquisition. He made a living working on microscope and telescope lens designs, collaborating with the famous physicist Christian Huygens. His most notable work is his philosophical treatise *"Ethics"*.

Closer to our times, we have Noble Prize Physicists like Claude Cohen-Tannoudji and Serge Haroche. Cohen-Tannoudji was born in *Constantine, Algeria*. His family had moved to Algeria in the 16th century after having fled Spain during the Inquisition. Cohen Tannoudji won the Nobel Prize in Physics in 1997. Serge Haroche was born in *Casablanca, Morocco*. He came from a Jewish family with mixed Sephardi and Ashkenazi origins. He was awarded the Nobel Prize in Physics in 2012, for his work on the fundamentals of Quantum Mechanics. His experiments succeeded in bringing alive the famous *"Schrodinger cat"*.

The Jewish diaspora before the 20th century

While Sephardic Jews originated in Western Europe (Portugal and Spain), Ashkenazi Jews originated in Central and Eastern Europe. And both branches originated from the ancient Jews who lived in the Land of Israel, who first dispersed along the Mediterranean Sea and from there to Western and Central Europe. The third branch of Jews are the Mizrahi, or Middle Eastern, Jews in countries such as Iraq, Syria and Yemen. The dispersal of the Jews stemmed mainly from the fact that the Jews were a small people living in a strategic point: The transit point between three continents, Asia, Africa and Europe. All the great powers of all time tried to take over this crossing point: Babylonians, Greeks and Romans first, and then, from the 7th century, Arabs, who spread from Mecca, Saudi Arabia, to the Mediterranean countries in Africa, and as far as everything that came their way, including Spain. It can be said that, because they were a small people, the Jews were carried by the wind, and some of these winds were quite strong and they ended up everywhere.

Who are the Mizrahi ('Oriental' or 'Middle East') Jews?

Perhaps the most known **Mizrahi Jews** are the *Babylonian Jews.* Their origin dates from the times when the Babylonian Empire conquered the first Kingdom of Judea (the one founded by the biblical Jewish kings Saul, David and Solomon) and destroyed their Temple in Jerusalem, in year 586 BCE. The Babylonians had a unique way to conquer lands, especially those inhabited by rebellious people: they captured the intellectual elite and transplanted it to Babylonia (*what is today* **Iraq**), leaving the conquered land without leaders. In 1950 there were 125,000-160,000 Jews in Iraq. One year later, in 1951 – 2,500 years of the Jewish community in Iraq came to an abrupt end: almost all were forced to leave, totally dispossessed of everything they had.

The most notable contribution of the Babylonian Jews was the *Talmud*, completed about the year 500 CE, an encyclopedic collection of the teachings and opinions of thousands of rabbis on a large variety of subjects covering all the aspects of Jewish life, including philosophy, religious customs and folklore. The *Talmud* was later studied by Jews all over the world: I studied parts of the Talmud when I was a teenager and attended a secular Jewish day-school in Argentina. This Jewish school occupied the whole second floor of the AMIA building in Buenos Aires. The AMIA was located *en la calle* Pasteur, in the center of Buenos Aires, three blocks away from the *Facultad de Medicina* of the Buenos Aires University.

The AMIA – a five story building housing also the IWO library in its fourth floor, a large library of Jewish books I used to visit – was completely destroyed by a bomb in year 1994, killing 85 people and injuring hundreds. The perpetrators, linked to the Iranian regime, were never brought to Justice, most probably because they were aided by some members of the military intelligence services of Argentina, well known for not liking the Jews.

The Ashkenazi Jews

Yiddish was the daily language spoken by the Ashkenazi Jews in Europe. It was the language spoken at home by my parents. And, as other Jewish kids in Argentina, I learnt Yiddish too. When I was a teenager, I enjoyed reading the hilarious stories of Sholem Aleichem in their original language, Yiddish. Everyone knows today Sholem Aleichem's story of *"Tevye and his daughters"*, made famous by the Broadway production of *"Fiddler on the Roof"*. The list of Ashkenazi Jews that contributed to the arts and sciences is quite long: I will only name a few. George Gershwin, born in New York in 1898, was the son of Ashkenazi Jews from Eastern Europe. He was a classically trained musician with *"jazzy"* inclinations. His *"Rhapsody in Blue"*, *"An American in Paris"* and his opera *"Porgy and Bess"* have delighted audiences all over the world. Arthur Miller was born in Harlem, New York, in 1915, the son of Ashkenazi Jews from Poland. His novel *"Death of a Salesman"* is a classic of American literature. Ashkenazi Jews have also had their share of great scholars. One of them was Jonas Salk. Salk was born in New York city, in 1914, a son of Ashkenazi Jews. He developed the first successful polio vaccine that helped eradicate poliomyelitis from the world. Another famous Ashkenazi Jew was the Physicist Albert Einstein, born in Germany. In 1933, with the rise of Nazism and the *"Boycott the Jews"* campaign launched that year in Germany, he left that country for good and moved to the US. Everyone knows Einstein because his equations of General Relativity predicted the Big Bang origin of the Universe and the existence of Black Holes, stars with such a powerful gravitational attraction that not even light can escape from them (so they appear as black holes in the sky).

For centuries Ladino and Yiddish were the daily languages spoken by Sephardi and Ashkenazi Jews in the Diaspora. Both Sephardi and Ashkenazi Jews shared a third language, Hebrew, which was used for sacred matters: prayers at the synagogues and the study of the *Bible* – the written history, philosophy and poetry of the ancient Jews living in the Land of Israel.

There is one interesting difference between Ladino and Yiddish: whereas spoken Ladino is "old spoken Spanish language from centuries ago" and spoken Yiddish is "old spoken German language from centuries ago", they differ essentially in the *written* language: written Ladino just uses the letters of the Spanish alphabet (which makes Ladino plainly identical to the old Spanish language, both spoken and written) whereas written Yiddish uses the letters of the Hebrew alphabet. This made it easier for Yiddish speaking Jews to mix sacred and other original Hebrew words with secular old-German words during their daily common life conversations: Ashkenazi Jews used to "spike" Yiddish in their secular conversations with plain Hebrew words. Words like *"chutzpah" (audacity)* that you frequently hear from Ashkenazi Jews made even their way into the gentile English-speaking people, like when one says: *"You can't help but admire the sheer chutzpah of the man"*. *"Chutzpah"* is not a Yiddish word: *it is plain original Hebrew!*

Jews in Modern Times

Ladino and Yiddish literature are part of the great *secular* Jewish culture, as well as it is the modern secular Hebrew literature renovated and created by writers and poets in Israel, like Aharon Megged and Amos Oz. Megged and Oz were both Ashkenazi Jews. I still remember the misty atmosphere of Jerusalem, the city in the mountains, described by Amos Oz in his romantic novel *"My Michael" ("Mijael Sheli", in Hebrew, as pronounced in Spanish)*, and the sense of disenchantment and disillusionment as Israelis' pioneering and sacrificial spirit evaporated as life returned to "normal" at the end of Israel's 1948 war of independence, described in Aharon Megged's short story *"Bountiful rain" ("Gueshem Nedavot", in Hebrew, as pronounced in Spanish)*. I read both the novel and the short story in their original Hebrew when I lived in Argentina. One of Israel's past Presidents, Yitzhak Navon, was a Sephardi Jew. Navon was born in Jerusalem, and belonged to a Sephardi family living in Israel since the 17th century. He composed two musical plays based on Sephardi folklore: *"Sephardic Romancero"* and *"Sephardic Garden"*. And, of course, we have the novelist Agnon, who in 1966 was awarded the Nobel Prize in Literature. For understandable reasons, both the Yiddish and Ladino usage in Israel declined, in favor of the unifying Hebrew language, known to both Sephardi and Ashkenazi Jews.

It is estimated that more than 95% of the Jews living in the US fall into the two categories of Sephardi and Ashkenazi Jews. Their integration in the US society, a long process that began in the 17th century, with the first Sephardi Jews arriving in New York and accelerated massively at the end of the 19th century, with the arrival of the Ashkenazi Jews fleeing the pogroms and the extreme poverty in Eastern Europe, is quite complete: both Sephardi and Ashkenazi Jews feel that the US is the land where – if you work hard enough – your dreams will come true, and is the place where Jews and their children can feel safe (until quite recently, of course).

Less can be said about the integration of the tens of thousands of Sephardi and Mizrahi Jews that lately arrived from the Arab countries following the 1948-1967 Israeli-Arab wars. Perhaps, they – as many other new immigrants from many other countries to the US – would prefer to be defined as *"people of color"*, with the advantages that this category lately offers to their advancement in the US education system and society. Some in this community might believe that the present version of the "Ethnic Studies Model Curriculum" (March 2021) in California is good for Jews. They are naïve and wrong. It only makes the Jews more vulnerable, by separating and trying to differentiate between a minority of recently arrived *"Jews of color"* (the *"good"* Jews, worth of protection and encouragement) and all the *"other Jews", the "European" white Jews,* Sephardi and Ashkenazi, integrated long ago in the US society, who should repent for their whiteness. And, of course, the Jews living in Israel, who should be boycotted.

A Jew is a Jew, and it does not matter whether he/she claims to come from Spain, Germany, Russia, Morocco, Libya, Syria or Israel. Antisemitic people do not care about these minor details.

Who am I?

This "*Brief History of the Jewish People*" would not be complete if a short background of the writer and his personal story is not given too. It adds perspective. Here it is:

I was born in Buenos Aires, Argentina. I do not know much about my parents, except that they were kind to me. I knew that my father, Isaac, had been an orphan from young age and lived with his uncles in a small town of Ukraine, Eastern Europe. I had heard that when he was about 16 years old, he escaped Ukraine crossing a dangerous river. He ended up somewhere in Western Europe and from there took a ship to Uruguay, a small country next to Argentina: Uruguay had a liberal policy regarding migrants from Eastern Europe. Shortly afterwards, he entered illegally Argentina in the mid 1920's and for some years worked as a *bracero* in the northern province of El Chaco, about 700 miles from Buenos Aires. Somehow, he ended up moving finally to Buenos Aires. He quietly became a naturalized citizen of Argentina about 30 years later, I think that thanks to some friends who helped him get the citizenship.

My mother, Clara, was born in Romania. Her whole family, her parents and about 10 children, emigrated to Argentina around the end of World War I, and upon arrival to Argentina they were taken directly from the ship to the remote province of La Pampa, to settle in a small town called Bernasconi, about 500 miles from Buenos Aires. They were very poor. I think they lived there from farming. The whole province of La Pampa was in the middle of nowhere, practically a desert. She went there to elementary school but I do not think that she finished school (not clear if there were real schools over there). With the passing of time, part of the family moved to the small coastal city of Bahia Blanca, others remained in Bernasconi, and my mother ended up finally in Buenos Aires.

I was born in Buenos Aires. For as far as I remember we always lived in the same small rented apartment in Buenos Aires, in the *barrio* of *Colegiales*. The street was called "14 de Julio" and the number was "1389". We lived in apartment "B".

I went to public schools, both for primary (kindergarten to K7) and secondary (K8-12) education. Catholicism was then the official religion in Argentina and in 3rd grade kids received catholic lessons at school. Since I was a Jewish kid, I was exempted and I was given books to read in silence in class during the catholic indoctrination lessons, while the teacher taught the catholic religion to the rest of the class. The books were about ethics and morality from the ancient Greek philosophers, many in the form of fables. I was fascinated by them. It was the first time I had the occasion to read this stuff. Then at home I began searching for similar books and I got hold of several old books with short stories by writers and philosophers. I think that, imperceptibly, it changed my life. I began loving reading books and it became a habit.

My teenage years were very simple: Monday-Friday mornings – public secondary school, afternoons – secular Jewish school for Hebrew Teachers, evenings – working at home on my homework at the dining table in the small kitchen. Saturday evenings going out with friends. Sundays were my free day. My last year at High School was particularly intense because I had to pack also an additional 90 minutes of daily classes between the public school in the mornings and the Jewish school in the afternoons, to attend a Preparatory Course (Geometry, Math, Chemistry and Physics), with exams, for admission at the Buenos Aires University offered at the *Facultad de Ingenieria*, located *en la Avenida Las Heras*, in the center of Buenos Aires (fortunately close to my Jewish school, so I could make it in time for the latter.) This last year was quite demanding: one Friday morning, while attending High School, the **History** teacher caught me slightly napping in class. To her question I answered: "*Because the lesson is boring*". I was a straight-A student. She was so startled that she did not react: usually, this impertinence would earn the student an *amonestación* and send him directly to the principal's office.

Hopefully, you will receive this brief 3,500 years of Jewish History more graciously.

Appendix 5: A sample of Jewish Literature and Music

A5.1: Isaac Leib Peretz

Isaac Leib Peretz (1852-1915), born in Poland into an orthodox Ashkenazi family, was one of the greatest Yiddish writers of all time. His short story *"If not higher"* is a classic Hasidic folktale.

Foreword

The story takes place in Nemirov, a town in Ukraine, similar to one of the hundreds of small villages in which the Jews lived in poor conditions in Eastern Europe at the end of the 19th century. In the background one can feel the tensions between two philosophical currents within Judaism: Hasidism and rabbinism.

Hasidism is a mystical Jewish movement that appeared in Eastern Europe around the 18th century, in reaction to the rigid academicism of rabbinical Judaism, the latter based on the study of the Talmud.

And now to the story:

If not higher

Early every Friday morning, at the time of the Penitential Prayers, the rabbi of Nemirov would vanish.

He was nowhere to be seen – neither in the synagogue nor in the two study houses nor at a minyan. And he was certainly not at home. His door stood open: whoever wished could go in and out; no one would steal from the rabbi. But not a living creature was within.

Where could the rabbi be? Where should he be? In heaven, no doubt. A rabbi has plenty of business to take care of just before the Days of Awe. Jews, God bless them, need livelihood, peace, health, and good matches. They want to be pious and good, but our sins are so great, and Satan of the thousand eyes watches the whole earth from one end to the other. What he sees, he reports; he denounces, informs. Who can help us if not the rabbi!

That's what the people thought.

But once a Litvak came, and he laughed. You know the Litvaks. They think little of the holy books but stuff themselves with Talmud and law. So, this Litvak points to a passage of the Gemara – it sticks in your eyes – where it is written that even Moses our Teacher did not ascend to heaven during this lifetime but remained suspended two and half feet below. Go argue with a Litvak!

So where can the rabbi be?

"That's not my business," said the Litvak, shrugging. Yet all the while – what a Litvak can do! – he is scheming to find out.

That same night, right after the evening prayers, the Litvak steals into the rabbi's room, slides under the rabbi's bed, and waits. He'll watch all night and discover where the rabbi vanishes and what he does during the Penitential Prayers.

Someone else might have gotten drowsy and fallen asleep, but a Litvak is never at a loss; he recites a whole tractate of the Talmud by heart.

At dawn he hears the call to prayers.

The rabbi has already been awake for a long time. The Litvak has heard him groaning for a whole hour.

Whoever has heard the rabbi of Nemirov groan knows how much sorrow for all Israel, how much suffering, lies in each groan. A man's heart might break, hearing it. But a Litvak is made of iron; he listens and remains where he is. The rabbi – long life to him! – lies on the bed, and the Litvak under the bed.

Then the Litvak hears the beds in the house begin to creak; he hears people jumping out of their beds, mumbling a few Jewish words, pouring water on their fingernails, banging doors. Everyone has left. It is again quiet and dark; a bit of light from the moon shines through the shutters.

(Afterward, the Litvak admitted that when he found himself alone with the rabbi a great fear took hold of him. Goose pimples spread across his skin, and the roots of his sidelocks pricked him like needles. A trifle: to be alone with the rabbi at the time of the Penitential Prayers! But a Litvak is stubborn. So he quivered like a fish in water and remained where he was.)

Finally, the rabbi – long life to him! – arises. First, he does what befits a Jew. Then he goes to the clothes closet and takes out a bundle of peasant clothes: linen trousers, high boots, a coat, a big felt hat, and a long, wide leather belt studded with brass nails. The rabbi gets dressed. From his coat pocket dangles the end of a heavy peasant rope.

The rabbi goes out, and the Litvak follows him.

On the way the rabbi stops in the kitchen, bends down, takes an ax from under the bed, puts it into his belt, and leaves the house. The Litvak trembles but continues to follow.

The hushed dread of the Days of Awe hangs over the dark streets. Every once in a while, a cry rises from some minyan reciting the Penitential Prayers, or from a sickbed. The rabbi hugs the sides of the streets, keeping to the shade of the houses. He glides from house to house, and the Litvak after him. The Litvak hears the sound of his heartbeats mingling with the sound of the rabbi's heavy steps. But he keeps on going and follows the rabbi to the outskirts of the town.

A small wood stands just outside the town.

The rabbi – long life to him! – enters the wood. He takes thirty or forty steps and stops by a small tree. The Litvak, overcome with amazement, watches the rabbi take the ax out of his belt and strike the tree. He hears the tree creak and fall. The rabbi chops the tree into logs and the logs into sticks. Then he makes a bundle of the wood and ties it with the rope in his pocket. He puts the bundle of wood on his back, shoves the ax back into his belt, and returns to the town.

He stops at a back street beside a small, broken-down shack and knocks at the window.

"Who is there?" asks a frightened voice. The Litvak recognizes it as the voice of a sick Jewish woman.

"I," answers the rabbi in the accent of a peasant.

"Who is I?"

Again, the rabbi answers in Russian. "Vassil."

"Who is Vassil, and what do you want?"

"I have wood to sell, very cheap." And not waiting for the woman's reply, he goes into the house.

The Litvak steals in after him. In the gray light of early morning, he sees a poor room with broken, miserable furnishings. A sick woman, wrapped in rags, lies on the bed. She complains bitterly. "Buy? How can I buy? Where will a poor widow get money?"

"I'll lend it to you," answers the supposed Vassil. "It's only six cents."

"And how will I ever pay you back?" asks the poor woman, groaning.

"Foolish one," says the rabbi reproachfully. "See, you are a poor, sick Jew, and I am ready to trust you with a little wood. I am sure you'll pay. While you, you have such a great and mighty God and you don't trust him for six cents."

"And who will kindle the fire?" asks the widow. "Have I the strength to get up? My son is at work."

"I'll kindle the fire," answers the rabbi.

As the rabbi put the wood into the oven he recited in a groan, the first portion of the Penitential Prayers.

As he kindled the fire and the wood burned brightly, he recited, a bit more joyously, the second portion of the Penitential Prayers. When the fire was set, he recited the third portion, and then he shut the stove.

The Litvak who saw all this became a disciple of the rabbi.

And ever after, when another disciple tells how the rabbi of Nemirov ascends to heaven at the time of the Penitential Prayers, the Litvak does not laugh. He only adds quietly, "If not higher."

(Source: *"The I. L. Peretz Reader"* by I. L. Peretz (Author), Ruth Wise (Editor). Translation to English by Marie Syrkin)

Lexicon

A Litvak: a Lithuanian Jew, stereotyped in Yiddish folktales as extremely rational

Talmud: the body of Jewish civil laws

Gemara: rabbinical commentaries of the Talmud

Minyan: a quorum of ten men over the age of 13 required for a traditional Jewish public worship

Days of Awe: the ten days of repentance and renewal between the Jewish New Year and Yom Kippur, the Day of Atonement

Sidelock: a long curl of hair that is worn hanging down at the side of the head by some Jewish men.

A5.2: Elias Canetti

Elias Canetti (1905-1994) was born into a Ladino-speaking Sephardic family in Ruschuk, Bulgaria. He won the Nobel Prize for Literature in 1981. The following, *"Family Pride"*, is a chapter of his book *"The Tongue Set Free: Remembrance of a European Childhood"*:

Family Pride

Ruschuk, on the lower Danube, where I came into the world, was a marvelous city for a child, and if I say that Ruschuk is in Bulgaria, then I am giving an inadequate picture of it. For people of the most varied backgrounds lived there, on any one day you could hear seven or eight languages. Aside from the Bulgarians, who often came from the countryside, there were many Turks, who lived in their own neighborhood, and next to it was the neighborhood of the Sephardim, the Spanish Jews – our neighborhood. There were Greeks, Albanians, Armenians, Gypsies. From the opposite side of the Danube came Rumanians; my wet nurse, whom I no longer remember, was Rumanian. There were also Russians here and there.

As a child, I had no real grasp of this variety, but I never stopped feeling its effects. Some people have stuck in my memory only because they belonged to a particular ethnic group and wore a different costume from the others. Among the servants that we had in our home during the course of six years, there was a Circassian and later on an Armenian. My mother's best friend was Olga, a Russian woman. Once every week, Gypsies came into our courtyard, so many that they seemed like an entire nation; the terrors they struck in me will be discussed below.

Ruschuk was an old port on the Danube, which made it fairly significant. As a port, it had attracted people from all over, and the Danube was a constant topic of discussion. There were stories about the extraordinary years when the Danube froze over; about sleigh rides all the way across the ice to Rumania; about starving wolves at the heels of the sleigh horses.

Wolves were the first wild animals I heard about. In the fairy tales that the Bulgarian peasant girls told me, there were werewolves, and one night, my father terrorized me with a wolf mask on his face.

It would be hard to give a full picture of the colorful time of those early years in Ruschuk, the passions and the terrors. Anything I subsequently experienced had already happened in Ruschuk. There, the rest of the world was known as "Europe", and if someone sailed up the Danube to Vienna, people said he was going to Europe. Europe began where the Turkish Empire had once ended. Most of the Sephardim were still Turkish subjects. Life had always been good for them under the Turks, better than for the Christian Slavs in the Balkans. But since many Sephardim were well-to-do merchants, the new Bulgarian regime maintained good relations with them, and King Ferdinand, who ruled for a long time, was said to be a friend of the Jews.

The loyalties of the Sephardim were fairly complicated. They were pious Jews, for whom the life of their religious community was rather important. But they considered themselves a special brand of Jews, and that was because of their Spanish background. Through the centuries since their expulsion from Spain, the Spanish they spoke with one another had changed little. A few Turkish words had been absorbed, but they were recognizable as Turkish, and there were nearly always Spanish words for them. The first children's songs I heard were Spanish, I heard old Spanish *romances*; but the thing that was most powerful, and irresistible for a child, was a Spanish attitude. With naïve arrogance, the Sephardim looked down on other Jews; a word always charged with scorn was *Todesco*, meaning a German or Ashkenazi Jew. It would have been unthinkable to marry a *Todesca*, a Jewish woman of that background, and among the many families that I heard about or knew as a child in Rushchuk, I cannot recall a single case of such a mixed marriage. I wasn't even six years old when my grandfather warned me against such a misalliance in the future. But this general discrimination wasn't all. Among the Sephardim themselves, there were the "good families", which meant the ones that had been rich since way back. The proudest words one could hear about a person were: "Es de buena familia" – "he's coming from a good family." How often and ad nauseam did I hear that from my mother. When she enthused about the Viennese *Burgtheather* [National Theater of Austria in Vienna] and read Shakespeare with me, even later on, when she spoke about Strindberg [a Swedish writer and playwright], who became her favorite author, she had no scruples whatsoever about telling that she came from a good family, there was no better family around. Although the literatures of the civilized languages she knew became the true substance of her life, she never felt any contradiction between this passionate universality and the haughty family pride that she never stopped nourishing.

Even back in the period when I was utterly in her thrall (she opened all the doors of the intellect for me, and I followed her, blind and enthusiastic), I nevertheless noticed this contradiction, which tormented and bewildered me, and in countless conversations during that time of my adolescence I discussed the matter with her and reproached her, but it didn't make the slightest impression. Her pride had found its channels at an early point, moving through them steadfastly; but while I was still quite young, that narrow-mindedness, which I never understood in her, biased me against any arrogance of background. I cannot take people seriously if they have any sort of caste pride, I regard them as exotic but rather ludicrous animals. I catch myself having reverse prejudices against people who plume themselves on their lofty origin. The few times that I was friendly with aristocrats, I had to overlook their talking about it, and had they sensed what efforts this cost me, they would have forgone my friendship. All prejudices are caused by other prejudices, and the most frequent are those deriving from their opposites.

Furthermore, the caste in which my mother ranked herself was a caste of Spanish descent and also of money. In my family, and especially in hers, I saw what money does to people. I felt that those who were most willingly devoted to money were the worst. I got to know all the shades, from money-grubbing to paranoia. I saw brothers whose greed had led them to destroy one another in years of litigation, and who kept on litigating when there was no money left. They came from the same "good" family that my mother was so proud of. She witnessed all those things too, we often spoke about it. Her mind was penetrating; her knowledge of human nature had been schooled in the great works of world literature as well as in the experiences of her own life. She recognized the motives of the lunatic self-butchery her family was involved in; she could easily have penned a novel about it; but her pride in this same family remained unshaken. Had it been love, I could have readily understood it. But she didn't even love many of the protagonists, she was indignant at some, she had scorn for others, yet for the family as a whole, she felt nothing but pride.

Much later, I came to realize that I, translated to the greater dimensions of mankind, am exactly as she was. I have spent the best part of my life figuring out the wiles of man as he appears in the historical civilizations. I have examined and analyzed power as ruthlessly as my mother her family's litigations. There is almost nothing bad that I couldn't say about humans and humankind. And yet my pride in them is so great that there is only one thing I really hate: their enemy, death.

(Source: "*The Schocken book of modern Sephardic literature*", introductions and editor: Ilan Stavans)

Lexicon

Wet nurse: a woman who breastfeeds and cares for another's child

A5.3: Amos Oz

Amos Oz (1939-2018) was born in Jerusalem, Israel. He is considered one of the most prolific writers of Israel. His work has been translated into dozens of languages and was the recipient of many honors and awards. The following is a short fragment (the beginning of chapter 2) of his novel "*My Michael*", published in 1968.

Foreword

The story is told by Hannah, a young woman in the 1950's in Israel, trying to make sense of her life and find her place in a society emerging from a bloody war of independence, where men were highly valued.

The time in the initial scene is in the early 1950's, a few years after the end of Israel's war of independence. During 1949-1951 Israel had absorbed about 600,000 refugees from Europe and the Arab countries, doubling the original population it had in 1948. As a result of the war and the massive migration, the economic situation was dire, the country was very poor and the government had to institute a strict regimen of austerity. This explains the phrase at the beginning of chapter 2: "*Austerity regulations were still in force. We were given artificial coffee and tiny paper bags of sugar.*"

And here comes the story, the beginning of the second chapter in Oz's novel:

My Michael

My father often used to say: Strong people can do almost anything they want to do, but even the strongest cannot choose what they want to do. I am not particularly strong.

Michael and I arranged to meet the same evening in Café Atara in Ben Yehuda Street. Outside an absolute storm was raging, beating down furiously on the stone walls of Jerusalem.

Austerity regulations were still in force. We were given *ersatz* coffee and tiny paper bags of sugar. Michael made a joke about this, but his joke was not funny. He is not a witty man – and perhaps he could not tell it in an amusing way. I enjoyed his efforts; I was glad that I was causing him some exertion. It was because of me that he was coming out of his cocoon and trying to be amused and amusing. When I was nine I still used to wish I could grow up as a man instead of a woman. As a child I always played with boys and I always read boys' books. I used to wrestle, kick and climb. We lived in Kiryat Shmuel, on the edge of the suburb called Katamon. There was a derelict plot of land on a slope, covered with rocks and thistles and pieces of scrap-iron, and at the foot of the slope stood the house of the twins. The twins were Arabs, Halil and Haziz, the sons of Rashid Shahada. I was a princess and they were my bodyguards, I was a conqueror and they my officers, I was an explorer and they my native bearers, a captain and they my crew, a master-spy and they my henchmen. Together we would explore distant streets, prowl through the woods, hungry, panting, teasing orthodox children, stealing into the woods round St. Symeon's convent, calling the British policemen names. Giving chase and running away, hiding and suddenly dashing out. I ruled over the twins. It was a cold pleasure, so remote.

Michael said:

"You're a coy girl, aren't you?"

When we had finished drinking our coffee Michael took a pipe out of his overcoat pocket and put it on the table between us. I was wearing brown corduroy trousers and a chunky red sweater, such as girls at the University used to wear at that time to produce a casual effect. Michael remarked shyly that I had seemed more feminine that morning in the blue woolen dress. To him, at least.

"You seemed different this morning, too," I said.

Michael was wearing a grey overcoat. He did not take it off the whole time we sat in Café Atara. His cheeks were glowing from the bitter cold outside. His body was lean and angular. He picked up his unlit pipe and traced shapes with it on the table-cloth. His fingers, playing with the pipe, gave me a feeling of peace. Perhaps he had suddenly regretted his remark about my clothes; as if correcting a mistake, Michael said he thought I was a pretty girl. As he said it he stared fixedly at the pipe. I am not particularly strong, but I am stronger than this young man.

"Tell me about yourself," I said.

Michael said:

"I didn't' fight in the *Palmach*. I was in the signal corps. I was a wireless operator in the Carmeli Brigade."

Then he started talking about his father. Michael's father was a widower. He worked in the waterworks department of the Holon municipality.

Rashid Shahada, the twins' father, was a clerk in the technical department of the Jerusalem municipality under the British. He was a cultivated Arab, who behaved towards strangers like a waiter.

Michael told me that his father spent most of his salary on his education. Michael was an only child, and his father cherished high hopes for him. He refused to recognize that his son was an ordinary young man. For instance, he used to read the exercises which Michael wrote for his geology course with awe, commending them with such set phrases as: "This is very scientific work. Very thorough.". His father's greatest wish was for Michael to become a professor in Jerusalem, because his paternal grandfather had taught natural sciences in the Hebrew teachers' seminary in Grodno. He had been very well thought of. It would be nice, Michael's father thought, if the chain could pass on from one generation to another.

"A family isn't a relay-race, with a profession as the torch," I said.

"But I can't tell my father that," Michael said. "He's a sentimental man, and he uses Hebrew expressions in the way that people used to handle fragile pieces of precious china. Tell me something about your family now."

I told him that my father had died in 1943. He was a quiet man. He used to talk to people as if he had to appease them and purchase a sympathy he did not deserve. He had a radio and electrical business – sales and simple repairs. Since his death my mother lived at Kibbutz Nof Harim with my elder brother, Emanuel. "In the evenings she sits with Emanuel and his wife Rina, drinking tea and trying to teach their son manners, because his parents belong to a generation which despises good manners. All day she shuts herself up in a small room on the edge of the kibbutz reading Turgenev and Gorki in Russian, writing me letters in broken Hebrew, knitting and listening to the wireless. That blue dress you liked on me this morning – my mother knitted it."

Michael smiled.

"It might be nice for your mother and my father to meet. I'm sure they would find a lot to talk about. Not like us, Hannah – sitting here talking about our parents. Are you bored?" he asked anxiously, and as he asked he flinched, as if he had hurt himself in asking.

"No," I said. "No, I'm not bored. I like it here."

Michael asked whether I hadn't said that merely out of politeness. I insisted. I begged him to tell me more about his father. I said that I liked the way he talked.

Michael's father was an austere, unassuming man. He gave over his evenings voluntarily to running the Holon working men's club. Running? Arranging benches, filing chits, duplicating notices, picking up cigarette-ends after meetings. It might be nice if our parents could meet … Oh, he had already said that once. He apologized for repeating himself and boring me. What was I reading at the University? Archaeology?

I told him I lived in digs with an orthodox family in Achvah. In the mornings I worked as a teacher in Sarah Zeldin's kindergarten in Kerem Avraham. In the afternoons I attended lectures on Hebrew literature. But I was only a first-year student.

"Student rhymes with prudent." Straining to be witty, in his anxiety to avoid pauses in the conversation, Michael resorted to a play on words. But the point was not clear, and he tried to rephrase it. Suddenly he stopped talking and made a fresh, furious attempt at lighting his obstinate pipe. I enjoyed his discomfiture. At that time I was still repelled by the sight of the rough men my friends used to worship in those days: great bears of *Palmach*-men who used to tackle you with gushing torrent of deceptive kindness; thick-limbed tractor-drivers coming all dusty from the Negev like marauders carrying off the women of some captured city. I loved the embarrassment of the student Michael Gonen in Café Atara on a winter's night.

A famous scholar came into the café in the company of two women. Michael leant towards me to whisper his name in my ear. His lips may have brushed my hair. I said:

"I can see right through you. I can read your mind. You're saying to yourself: 'What's going to happen next? Where do we go from here?' Am I right?"

Michael reddened suddenly, like a child caught stealing sweets:

"I've never had a regular girlfriend before."

"Before?"

Thoughtfully Michael moved his empty cup. He looked at me. Deep down, underneath his meekness, a suppressed sneer lurked in his eyes.

"Till now."

(Source: Translation from Hebrew to English by Nicholas de Lange, in collaboration with Amos Oz)

Lexicon

Ersatz: (of a product) made or used as a substitute, typically an inferior one, for something else

Palmach: elite paramilitary unit before Israel's independence

Grodno: a city in Belarus, Europe

Kiryat Shmuel, Katamon, Achvah, Kerem Avraham: neighborhoods in Jerusalem

Holon: a city in the plains, next to Tel-Aviv

Negev: the southern desert of Israel

A5.4: Jacob Henry

Jacob Henry (1775-1847) had been elected in 1809 to be a legislator in the House of Commons of the state of North Carolina. At that time – barely a few years after the war of independence against the British – there were around only 2,000 Jews in America.

Another legislator, Hugh Mills, moved to oppose Jacob Henry serving in the Legislature because "he denies the divine authority of the New Testament, and refuses to take the oath prescribed by law for his qualification." At that time, the North Carolina constitution of 1776 forbade the holding of public office by those who denied "the truth of the Protestant religion" or "the divine authority either of the Old or New Testaments" or who hold "religious principles incompatible with the freedom and safety of the State." [see Reference at the end]

After a day of debate – and Henry's rousing speech, presented below – the House voted to reject Mills' recommendation and Henry retained his seat. Jacob Henry's speech was a milestone for religious rights throughout the country. It was widely reprinted and quoted in similar debates. The questions that Henry posed in his speech go to the core of the democratic experiment and demand that freedom of worship be an inalienable right.

And here comes Jacobs Henry's speech:

To the Honorable the Speaker, and members of the House of Commons:

I must confess that the resolution against me yesterday was quite unexpected, as I had a right to expect, that the Gentleman who introduced it, would have had the politeness to have given me notice of it.

The Gentleman has stated that I deny the divine authority of the Old and New Testaments.

However, Gentlemen, I know not the design of the Declaration of Rights made by the people of this State in the year '76 and one day before the Constitution, if it was not to consecrate certain great and fundamental rights and Principles, which even the Constitution cannot impair: For the 44th section of the latter instrument declares that the Declaration of Rights ought never to be violated on any pretense whatever. If there is any apparent difference between the two instruments they ought if possible be reconciled. But if there is a final repugnance between them, the Declaration of Rights must be considered paramount: For I believe that it [the Declaration of Rights] is to the Constitution as the Constitution is to a Law; it controls and directs it absolutely and conclusively. If then a belief in the Protestant religion is required by the Constitution to qualify a man for a seat in this House and such qualification is dispensed with by the Declaration of Rights, the provision of the Constitution must be altogether inoperative, as the language of the Bill of Rights is "that all men have a natural and unalienable right to worship Almighty God according to the dictates of their own consciences." It is undoubtedly a natural right, and when it is declared to be an unalienable one by the people in their sovereign and original capacity, any attempt to alienate it either by the Constitution or by law, mut be vain and fruitless.

It is difficult to conceive how such a provision crept into the Constitution unless it was from the difficulty the human mind feels in suddenly emancipating itself from fetters by which it has long been enchained: And how adverse it is to the feelings and manners of the *people* of the present day every Gentleman may satisfy himself by glancing at the Religious beliefs of the persons who fill the various civil offices in this State – There are Presbyterians, Lutherans, Calvinists, Mennonites, Baptists, Trinitarians and Unitarians. But as far as my observation extends, there are fewer Protestants in the strict sense of the word used by the Convention than of any other persuasion; for I supposed that they meant by it the Protestant religion as established by Law in England. For other persuasions we see houses of Worship in almost every part of the State, but very few for protestants; so few, that indeed I fear that the people of this State, would for some time, remain unrepresented in this House, if the clause of the Constitution is supposed to be in force. So far from believing in the truths of the 39 articles, I will venture to assert that a majority of the people have never read them.

If a man should hold religious principles incompatible with the freedom and safety of the State, I do not hesitate to pronounce that he should be excluded from the public Councils of the same; and I trust if I know myself no one would be more ready to aid and assist than myself. But I should really be at a loss to specify any known religious principles which are thus dangerous.

It is surely a question between a man and his Maker, and requires more than human attributes to pronounce which of the numerous Sects prevailing in the world is most acceptable to the Deity. If a man fulfills the duties of that religion which his education or his Conscience has pointed to him as the true one; no person, I hold, in this our land of liberty, has a right to arraign him at the bar of any inquisition – And the day I trust is long past when principles merely speculative were propagated by force, when the sincere and pious were made victims, and the light minded bribed into hypocrites.

The proud monuments of liberty knew that the purest homage man could render to the Almighty was in the sacrifice of his passions and in the performance of his duties; that the ruler of the universe would receive with equal benignity, the various offerings of man's adoration if they proceed from an humble spirit and sincere mind; that intolerance in matters of faith, had been from the earliest ages of the world, the severest torments by which mankind could be afflicted; and that governments were only concerned about the actions and conduct of man, and not his speculative notions.

Who among us feels himself so exalted above his fellows, as to have a right to dictate to them their mode of belief? Shall this free Country set an example of Persecution, which even the returning reason of enslaved Europe would not submit to? Will you bind the Conscience in Chains, and fasten conviction upon the mind, in spite of the conclusions of reason, and of those ties and habitudes which are blended with every pulsation of the heart? Are you prepared to plunge at once from the sublime heights of moral legislation, into the dark and gloomy caverns of superstitious ignorance? Will you drive from your shores and from the shelter of your constitutions, all who do not lay their oblations on the same altar, observe the same ritual, and subscribe to the same dogmas? If so, which amongst the various sects into which we are divided, shall be the favored one?

No Gentlemen, I should not insult your understandings, to suppose it possible that you could ever assent to such absurdities. For you all know that persecution in all its shapes and modifications, is contrary to the Genius of our Government, and the spirit of our laws; and that it can never produce any other effect, than to render men hypocrites or martyrs.

When Charles the fifth, Emperor of Germany, tired of the cares of Government, resigned his Crown to his son, he retired to a monastery, where he amused the evening of his life, in regulating the movements of watches, endeavoring to make a number keep the same time, but not being able to make any two go exactly alike, it led him to reflect upon the folly and crimes he had committed, in attempting the impossibility of making men think alike!!

Nothing is more easily demonstrated than that the Conduct alone is the subject of human laws, and that man ought to suffer civil disqualification for what he does and not for what he thinks.

The mind can receive laws only from him, of whose divine essence it is a portion; he alone can punish disobedience, for who else can know its movements; or estimate their merits? The religion I profess, inculcates every duty which man owes to his fellow men, it enjoins upon its votaries, the practice of every virtue, and the detestation of every vice; it teaches them to hope for the favor of Heaven exactly in proportion as their lives are directed by just, honorable and beneficent maxims – This then Gentlemen is my Creed; it was impressed upon my infant mind, it has been the director of my youth, the monitor of my manhood, and will I trust to be the Consolation of my old age. At any rates Gentlemen, I am sure that you cannot see, anything in this religion, to deprive me of my seat in this House. So far as relates to my life and conduct, the examination of these, I submit with cheerfulness to your candid and liberal construction. What may be the religion of those, who have made this objection against me, or whether they have any religion or not, I am unable to say. I have never considered it my duty to pry into the belief of my fellow citizens or neighbors, if their actions are upright and their conduct just, the rest is for their own consideration not for mine. I do not seek to make converts to my faith, whatever it may be esteemed in the eyes of my officious friend, nor do I exclude any man from my esteem or friendship, because he and I differ in that respect – The same charity therefore it is not unreasonable to expect will be extended to myself, because in all things that relate to the State and the duties of civil life, I am bound by the same obligations, with my fellow citizens; nor does any man subscribe more sincerely than myself to the maxim, "Whatever ye would that men should do unto [ye], do ye so even unto them, for such is the Law of the Prophets."

With the highest respect I remain Gentlemen yours respectfully

J. Henry

Reference

The 1776 Declaration of Rights and Constitution of the state of North Carolina are documents of historical interest. They are short and can be read at:

https://avalon.law.yale.edu/18th_century/nc07.asp

A5.5: Jewish music - the Eastern Mediterranean style

Bracha Zefira

Bracha Zefira (1910-1990) was a pioneering Israeli folk singer, songwriter, musicologist and actress. She was born in Jerusalem in 1910 in a family of Yemenite Jews. Her father had emigrated from Yemen in year 1887 and settled in a Yemenite neighborhood in Jerusalem.

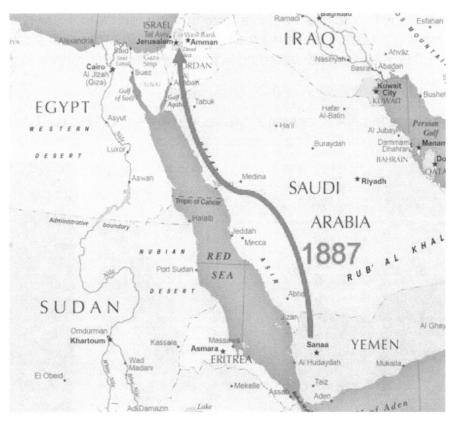

Figure 1: Bracha Zefira's father emigrated from Sana'a, Yemen's capital, to Jerusalem, in year 1887. At that time both Yemen and Jerusalem were part of the Ottoman Empire. (For pedagogical purposes a modern political map of the region is shown)

She brought Yemenite and other Mizrahi and Sephardi Jewish music into the musical life of the Jewish public at large, both in Israel, in Europe and the US. Her repertoire included more than 400 songs: Yemenite, Bukharan, Persian, Ladino and North African Jewish folk songs.

Her personal and musical path was unique. She was orphaned of both parents by the age of three: her mother died when she was born and her father died from typhus. She was raised by a succession of Mizrahi and Sephardi Jewish foster families in Jerusalem. She was gifted with a rich voice and a natural inclination to remember and annotate the melodies she was surrounded with in her youth. She was unique in that she sought the collaboration of the best classically-trained musicians, to incorporate the Mizrahi and Sephardi songs into the "serious" musical repertoire. She had a long relationship with the pianist Nahum Vardi, whom she met in Europe in 1929, while she was studying theater performance. She usually asked him to accompany her songs with improvisations at the piano. They ended up marrying. They divorced ten years later when he refused to accompany her songs with arrangements from other composers (instead of his own) …

Her work with classically-trained composers made possible the introduction of her repertoire into the classical concert arena. The interest was mutual: for them, Bracha Zefira was a walking encyclopedia of melodies and rhythms they were eager to integrate into their compositions.

There are not many recordings available from that era long ago. Here is a short one, with Zefira singing a Ladino melody accompanied with an orchestral arrangement by composer Paul Ben-Haim. The recording is from a public performance in year 1949:

https://www.youtube.com/watch?v=804o4ROyu7M

(Click on the above hyperlink, or type it: the image below is only to confirm you arrived at the right place)

Streets in Jerusalem and other cities in Israel carry her name and the Israeli Post Office issued a commemorative stamp of her, which is shown in the video.

Bracha Zefira, together with the composer Paul Ben-Haim, were pioneers of the "*Eastern Mediterranean*" or "*Israeli*" style in music that began developing in the 1930s and remained in a prominent position well into the late 1950s.

Lexicon:

Bucharan Jews: Their name comes from the former Central Asian Emirate of Bukhara (now Uzbekistan). The Bucharan Jews called themselves "*Bnei Israel*" or "*Children of Israel*", to indicate that their ancestors came from the ancient biblical *Kingdom of Israel,* located in the hills and mountains of Samaria (today's northern and central West

Bank), who were taken in captivity by the Assyrians around 720 BCE. The first Bucharan Jews that migrated back to Israel arrived in the 1870s and 1880s, establishing the Bukharim quarter, or neighborhood, in Jerusalem. Today, about 160,000 Bucharan Jews live in Israel.

Persian Jews: Are the descendants of Jews who were historically associated with the Persian Empire (now Iran), dating back to biblical times. Many Persian Jews began arriving back to Israel in the early 1900s. Today, there are about 200,000-250,000 Persian Jews living in Israel.

Paul Ben-Haim

Paul Ben-Haim (1897-1984), was born in Germany. He was an accomplished pianist, composer and orchestra conductor. In 1924 he was appointed as Kapellmeister and choir conductor at the Augsburg Stadttheater, a position previously held by both Gustav Mahler and Richard Strauss. Over seven years he conducted some 40 operas and operettas, until he lost this position with the rise of the Nazism. In 1933, with the beginning of the "*Boycott the Jews*" campaign in Germany, he emigrated to Israel, where he Hebraized his name to Paul Ben-Haim (his birth name was Paul Frankenburger.) His sister, Rosa, perished in Auschwitz's concentration camp.

He composed his first symphony in 1939-1940. This was the first symphony composed in the Land of Israel. He dedicated it to the Israeli Philharmonic Orchestra (then known as the "Palestine Orchestra", before the Jewish independence from the British), that had been founded a mere three years before in Tel-Aviv, in 1936.

It is a magnificent symphony, composed in classical tonal style. The symphony is thirty minutes long and has three movements. Its first movement, "*Allegro energico*", evokes the tragedy unfolding in Europe, with the beginning of World War II. It has a short basic motif that dominates the whole movement, similar to Beethoven's main motif in the first movement of his 5th symphony. The second movement, "*Molto calmo e cantabile*", is pastoral, and elegiac and lyrical at times. The final movement, "*Presto con fuoco*", is like a whirlwind of rhythm, with alternating short respites.

Click on the following link to listen to a recent rendition by the Symphony Orchestra of the Berlin University of the Arts:

https://www.youtube.com/watch?v=jc_xiU8h_bE

(Click on the above hyperlink, or type it: the image that follows below is only to confirm you arrived at the right place)

Prior to the 1930s there was no "serious" concert music in Palestine. The arrival during this decade of many classically-trained musicians fleeing the horrors of Nazism, changed this completely. In Western Europe contemporary music had become mainly atonal, did not know national boundaries nor were their composers interested in including local, national, characteristics: listening to this music one could never tell if the composer lived in Europe or in America. But another trend also developed, represented by musicians like Bela Bartok (Hungary, 1881-1945) and Zoltan Kodaly (Hungary, 1882-1967), where ethnic, folk-music, elements were integrated in their works.

The newly arrived Jewish musicians from Europe faced the same dilemma, but to them the decision was clear: they had fled the horrors of Europe, they wanted to bury and forget anything related to that continent, they had come to a new country, Eretz Israel (the Land of Israel) and they eagerly began looking to integrate elements of the Eastern culture into their music. They found these elements in the Mizrahi and Sephardi Jewish songs and melodies. But how to integrate them into the "serious" music? These songs and melodies were based on scales different from the Western scales one finds in the classical music of Mozart and Beethoven. The solution? Go back to the ancient pre-classical music principles: modal music. Modal-based music was very versatile and in the same way that one could write music using the Mixolydian, Dorian and Lydian modes, these musicians could also integrate the "Yemenite" and "Ladino" scales into "serious" orchestral music. And so was born the "*Eastern Mediterranean*" Israeli style that became the hegemonic style of writing music in Israel, from the 1940s till the 1960s.

The influence of Bracha Zefira and her popular melodies and style can be found in Paul Ben-Haim's orchestral suite "*From Israel*", composed in 1951.

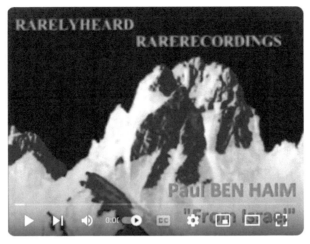

Paul Ben Haim "From Israel"

The suite consists of five movements or dances: 1) Prologue, 2) Song of Songs, 3) Yemenite Melody, 4) Siesta, and 5) Celebration. You can listen to this suite at:

https://www.youtube.com/watch?v=Ec8ZdXDyhuY

(*Lexicon*: "siesta" is a Ladino/Spanish word literally meaning "*a light rest or sleep*", taken usually in the early afternoon, after a meal. May also have the connotation of a light and pleasant "dream" in the middle of the day. You will understand the mood when you will listen to the music.)

Another classic example of this "Eastern Mediterranean" Israeli style – this time in the realm of sacred music – is Paul Ben-Haim's piece "*Kabbalat Shabbat*". If you love Johan Sebastian Bach's sacred music, his cantatas and oratorios, you will enjoy also Ben-Haim's "*Kabbalat Shabbat*", although it sounds very different from Bach's music because of its use of modal composition. "*Kabbalat Shabbat*" was first performed in the Lincoln Center Symphony Hall in New York, in year 1968. The duration of the piece is about 40 minutes and it consists of 15 short movements (detailed below).

Use the following link to listen to the whole piece:

https://www.youtube.com/watch?v=9kAa2rJB8Ok&list=OLAK5uy_mQANI_9jWlnDrVj CKoMF3JZTMQ4XAU0OM

The image that follows is to help you confirm that you got to the right place:

(*Note*: the 3:16 in the above image indicates the duration of the first movement, "Introduction and Chorus". The video will switch automatically from one movement to the next)

And here is the detail of the fifteen movements:

1) Introduction and Chorus: Psalm 98

2) Lighting of the Sabbath Candles

3) Sabbath Hymn, "L'kha dodi"

4) Barechu (Praise ye the Lord)

5) Sh'ma Yisrael

6) Ve-ahav'ta (Thou Shalt Love)

7) Mi khamokha (Who is Like unto Thee)

8) Ve-shamru (They Shall Keep the Sabbath)

9) Hashkivenu

10) Shalom rav al Yisrael, "Grant us Peace"

11) Yih'yu le-ratson (Guide me)

12) Kiddush

13) Adoration

14) Bayom ha-hu (On that Day)

15) Concluding Hymn and Benediction, "Adon olam"

If you want a detailed analysis of which and how the modal scales were used in this composition, I refer you to the doctoral dissertation by Holly Dalrymple [1].

Reference

[1] Holly Dalrymple, "*From Germany to Palestine: a comparison of two choral works by Paul Ben-Haim – Joram and Kabbalat Shabbat*", University of North Texas, August 2013. A link to download this dissertation is:

https://digital.library.unt.edu/ark:/67531/metadc500208/

Lesson 6
A ray of hope

President Donald J. Trump, Minister of Foreign Affairs of Bahrain Dr. Abdullatif bin Rashid Al-Zayani, Israeli Prime Minister Benjamin Netanyahu and Minister of Foreign Affairs for the United Arab Emirates Abdullah bin Zayed Al Nahyan sign the Abraham Accords, September 15, 2020, on the South Lawn of the White House. (Official White House Photo by Shealah Craighead)

In December 2020, Morocco joined the Abraham Accords.

The Abraham Accords are peace treaties between Israel and Bahrain, the United Arab Emirates (UAE) and Morocco.

The Abraham Accords

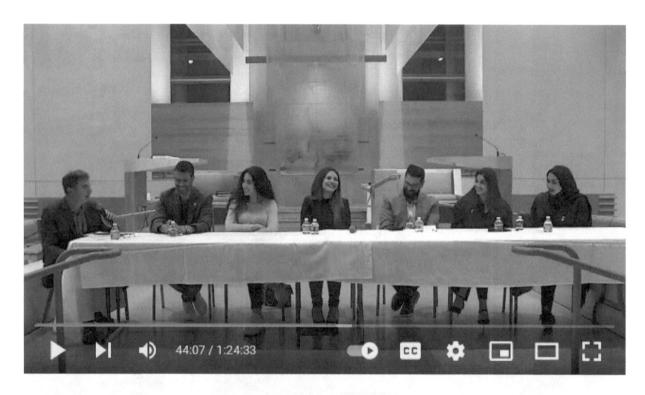

How The Abraham Accords Are Changing The Face Of The Middle East

Enabling Dialog and Inclusiveness

Preface

On November 11th, 2021, the Jewish Federation of Sacramento, California, hosted a round table with a delegation of *Sharaka*. *Sharaka* is an organization of young leaders from the United Arab Emirates, Bahrain, Morocco and Israel. It was founded following the *Abraham Accords* in 2020 to foster cooperation between Israel and the Arab world ("sharaka" means "partnership" in Arabic). The Abraham Accords are peace treaties normalizing diplomatic relations between Israel and the United Arab Emirates, Bahrain and Morocco.

There is a YouTube video of the round table, titled "***How the Abraham Accords are changing the face of the Middle East***":

https://www.youtube.com/watch?v=E8grK2_5iBg&t=1s

Having this round table in additional formats will help reaching to wider audiences. My transcription is based on the original video. I apologize to the panelists and moderator for any omissions and mistakes that I could have generated during the transcription.

Jaime Kardontchik, PhD (Physics)

Silicon Valley, California

December 1st, 2021

Introduction

Bruce Pomer: *I am the President of the Jewish Federation of the Sacramento Region. We are pleased that you are here tonight for our program "How the Abraham Accords are changing the face of the Middle East".*

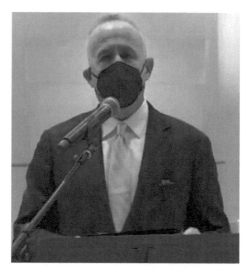

Darell Steinberg, Mayor of Sacramento, California: *Good evening and welcome. It is an honor to be here. I think the world is desperate for hope. The "Abraham Accords" are a series of treaties normalizing diplomatic relations between Israel and the United Arab Emirates, Bahrain and Morocco. These agreements were negotiated in 2020 with the active assistance of the United States. And the United States government is seeking today an expansion of the normalization to other countries. Let us have a great evening.*

Ben-Dror Yemini [*]: I have to admit that being here and sitting here together with this kind of delegation is a dream coming true, because I am older enough to know that some ten or twenty years ago, we could not even dream about something of this kind. My personal story with the peace process, the peace making with the Arab countries, begins many, many years ago, when I went to meet Yasser Arafat, before the Oslo Accords, in Tunisia. Years went on and, unfortunately, peace did not come. Now we see a change. Now we see a change in the Arab world, because all the way, we always had, as human beings, we had to choose between two directions. One direction is that people criticize Israel. Fair enough. I do it myself, as a journalist. In times I do not like the policies of my government. But it is going much further. In many times we are speaking about demonization of Israel, we are speaking about BDS [boycott], we are speaking about people that they don't even recognize the right of Israel to exist. This is one way. The other way is to humanize the other side. To accept the other side. Not to say that it is a monster. And the whole idea of the "Abraham Accords" is that we accept the other. People sometimes do not understand the meaning, the real meaning of the "Abraham Accords", because the impact of the accords is much bigger than what we think. I will give you just one example: following the Abraham Accords there was a survey in the Arab world, by the Zogby Institute, a Washington-based institute. They were asked, the Arabs in the Arab countries: "*Are you in favor of normalization with Israel, even without peace with the Palestinians?*". And surprise, surprise: Most of the Arabs in the Gulf countries, but not only in the Gulf countries, in Saudi Arabia, in Jordan, in Egypt, are in favor of normalization and peace with Israel. It is because of the Abraham Accords. Now, from one hand we have this kind of coalition of what? Of Hamas, of Iran, of people around the world, *even in the West* – and I have to put it on the table – that are against the existence of Israel, that they are in favor of BDS, that they are in favor of hatred. From the other side, we have now Arabs and Jews, supporting peace and reconciliation. So, it is a dream coming true. Now, the big question is, who is going to win? The axis of Iran and BDS and Hamas? Or the axis of those who are striving for peace and reconciliation and mutual recognition? And, yes, also peace with the Palestinians: Of course, we need it. But the way to achieve peace with the Palestinians is by this kind of activities we see tonight. It is by recognition; it is by reconciliation. Not by hatred. Not by BDS. Not by boycott, not by Iran and jihad. So, I am so glad to be here, because there is a hope that from the two coalitions, the coalition of peace and reconciliation is going to win. And we have to work on it, all of us together.

[*] Ben-Dror Yemini is a journalist from the Israeli newspaper Yedioth Ahronoth, author of the book "*Industry of Lies: Media, Academia and the Israeli-Arab Conflict*"

The panel

44:07 / 1:24:33

How The Abraham Accords Are Changing The Face Of The Middle East

The six panelists were (from right to left) Fatema Al Harbi (Bahrain), Lorena Khateeb (Israeli Arab), Dan Feferman (Israeli Jew), Hayvi Bouzo (Syria), Chama Mechtaly (Morocco) and Omar Al Busaidy (United Arab Emirates).

The moderator of the panel (left) was Don Gilbert, Vice-President of the Jewish Federation of Sacramento, California.

Fatema Al Harbi is a published fiction writer and cultural activist, vice-chair of Sharaka, Bahrain.

Lorena Khateeb is an Israeli Arab Druze. She works at the Israeli Foreign Ministry in the Department of Digital Diplomacy and is a founding member of Sharaka.

Dan Feferman is an Israeli-American author, speaker and co-host of the podcast "*Jewanced*". He is the Director of Communications, Global Affairs, at Sharaka.

Hayvi Bouzo is a Syrian born television journalist of Kurdish descent, the Washington DC bureau chief for the *Orient News* and main host of the political television show "*The Axis*".

Chama Mechtaly, born in Morocco, is the founder and CEO of "*Moors & Saints*". She is a jeweler designer, a visual artist and advocate for interfaith dialogue.

Omar Al Busaidy is a Fulbright Scholar, the economic affairs liaison at the United Arab Emirates consulate in New York, and CEO of Sharaka.

The round table

Don Gilbert: Thank you for being here, and welcome to Sacramento. I will ask the first question of all of you: How each of you became involved in this effort to engage in public discussion, and the impact of the Abraham Accords on your lives and on your fellow citizens in your respective countries? Maybe we will start with Fatema and work our way down.

Fatema Al Harbi: Hello everyone, it is a pleasure to be here. Thankfully, I have been raised in a very open-minded family, I have been taught to accept all religions and backgrounds since I was a kid. I have studied also abroad in Australia, so I am used to being around people from all backgrounds and ethnic groups. When the Abraham Accords were announced in September last year, I was so happy that the impossible is possible, so I have been tweeting and talking about this with friends and family. Just one month later, Sharaka approached me and asked me if I wanted to visit Israel. "*Yes, of course*", I answered. I wanted to know the unknown. People In Bahrain have been taught that Israel is the evil in the Middle East. I wanted to go and see, if it was really evil in real life or not. I did not want to hear about this: I wanted to see it by myself. Thankfully, I was the first Bahraini youth non-governmental official to visit Israel after the Abraham Accords. And what I saw was completely the opposite. There was nothing evil about Israel. People were living their lives normally, filled with life and joy and living with their Muslim brothers and sisters. I loved it. It Is not like the media shows us. And people in Bahrain were shocked when I told them and they started asking me questions. They had never seen Israel before in a good way, without any filters. People were happy about it and they kept asking me how can they get there as soon as possible. They wanted to see it as I saw it. So, this was the beginning for me.

Lorena Khateeb: Good evening. It is an honor and pleasure. I am from the North of Israel, Galilee. I am a Druze, an Israeli Arab. I am one of the co-founders of Sharaka. I work at the Israeli Foreign Ministry, within the Department of Digital Diplomacy. I also work at the Arabic language television: we reach daily more than ten million followers and people from all over the Arab world. I am also project manager at the organization "Together – Vouch for Each Other" that connects the Israeli-Arab society to the Israeli society. Since 1956, when the leaders of the Druze community signed an agreement with the government that every eighteenth Druze citizen must join the army, except women and religious people, I decided to do one year of national service within the Druze community in order to bring the Druze community into the Israeli society. Within my duties during the reserve service, I went with a delegation to the Holocaust Remembrance Center, *Yad Vashem*: I was the only Israeli-Arab between like about fifty Palestinians and Jews. I faced a lot of misconceptions about Israel. I felt that I am responsible for doing something as an Israeli Arab. I started to advocate for Israel especially in my native language, in Arabic. I saw that people are very curious to get to know Israel. I was dedicated to building ties with our new friends in the Arab countries and all over the world that want to know more about Israel. So, this is how all my activities began.

Hayvi Bouzo: Thank you so much. We are very happy to be here. I was born in Damascus, Syria, and raised there. My mother was born and grew up in the Jewish quarter in Aleppo. We grew up hearing the Jewish stories about the Jewish community in Aleppo, the ancient Jewish community that was basically pushed out of Syria, systematically. My mom told us very sad and heartbreaking stories about her witnessing her friends and neighbors being basically forced out, literally. My father was from Damascus – I am also party Kurdish, and my mother is half Turkish, it is a mixture, the way the Middle East is. My father told us about the Jewish quarter in Damascus, in the old city of Damascus inside of the fence, where only a few neighborhoods are there, because it is really ancient in the city, before other communities came, including Arabs, Islam, and all of that. This part of our history in the Middle East – and this includes of course Jerusalem and the Land of Israel – is not being taught by anybody in the region in Arabic language, so you do not know about the indigenousness of the Jewish people inside of the Middle East. So, growing up and wanting to be a journalist and wanting to share stories and educate people – because that is what journalists should do – I actually had a TV show where I started talking about things from a different narrative. I had a rabbi who was helping Syrian refugees after the Syrian war and I also had a program about "*The good neighbor*" project that Israel was doing to help Syrians who were actually displaced and were stuck at the Israeli border: hundreds of thousands of Syrians families were being help. And that is basically why people started really wondering and asking questions about Israel and about the Jewish history. Things that were hidden were now being uncovered. But thanks to the Abraham Accords we have finally governments who are doing the extra steps and allowing people to safely connect and be together and have these conversations. The difference between the Abraham Accords and previous peace agreements between Israel with Egypt and Jordan, is that these previous peace agreements did not allow for these conversations. Because we saw, for example, a very famous Egyptian writer,

114

Ali Salem, who when he went to visit Israel, he was punished and marginalized in Egypt. But the Abraham Accords are different, because now these governments, Arab governments, are actually promoting people to people conversations and dialog. And this is the path forward for the Middle East. There is no other solution but peace. I definitely think that it is also really important that you are here today and that we are having this conversation in the United States too, because unfortunately – due to the polarization in the political sphere in the US – this has also affected how people look at peace in the Middle East, and kind of see it from an angle of what is happening here in the United States, which is incorrect, because the polarizations in the US and in the Middle East are unrelated and have nothing to do with each other. I had recently conversations on a TV show – after the Abraham Accords – with people talking about interreligious dialog. And people were happy to just sharing and having questions and wanting to learn. And this is just the beginning, the beginning of having and creating a new Middle East, where there is peace and prosperity.

Chama Mechtaly: Thank you so much for having us. I grew up in Casablanca, Morocco, in a Muslim family, although my grandfather from my father's side came from a Jewish family and married a Muslim woman. Growing up, I was nurtured by these stories of interfaith dialog that are deeply entrenched in the Moroccan society that my father was telling me about. Whereas at home there was a sort of longing and beautiful story telling about Muslim-Jewish dialog and interfaith, when I stepped into the public space and when I went to school, I noticed that Jewish history in Morocco was not taught, was not represented in the media, so very early on I started advocating for the inclusion of that history in public schools. I was the first person to advocate for the inclusion of the indigenous Jewish history in the Moroccan curriculum. Later on, I went to Brandeis University in Massachusetts for undergrad. I studied international relations and conflict resolution with the folks in the Middle East and I took a minor in Hebrew. The latter was also my introduction to the Ashkenazi Jewry and exposed me to a lot of the differences and nuances in the Jewish world. Studying at Brandeis exposed me also to some of the nuances within the Muslim world and gave me an understanding on how to bridge all these cultures and identities not just in the East but also in the West. After Brandeis, I worked in refugee advocacy in the Mediterranean, and worked in the Moroccan parliament in the division of international affairs and cooperation. I moved to Dubai five years ago where I set up a start-up using Moorish design and architecture as a way of telling the stories of coexistence, interfaith dialog and cultural syncretism, specifically between Islam and Judaism, mapping their similarities across sacred sites all over the world, but also related to other faiths too, whether they are Jewish, or Muslim or Christian. For example, we had a collection that was inspired by a mosque that was built a thousand years ago in Cairo where we found stars of David, and the university that was built right next to this mosque was actually founded by a Jewish man originally from Iraq who ended up converting to Islam. So, I sought to bring the complexity of the picture and dismantle the otherness that existed for a long time across decades of media manipulation and misinformation about the other side. I have done that before moving into the UAE, specifically focusing on arts and visual arts, painting in ways that represent Jewish history in the Middle East and North Africa and setting up exhibitions in academic spaces also, where I would use arts to kind of dismantle that otherness. For example, I had a solo exhibition in Boston in 2012 and I had a lot of people come over form the Muslim diaspora in the Massachusetts area and they noticed I had these paintings of Jewish women on the wall and they looked at their attire and the jewelry and everything and their faces, and they said "*how did you get the picture of my grandmother*?". And I would say, "*but she is Jewish, so what do you think?*" So slowly they would start to dismantle those barriers of otherness that they had built up over the years. One thing I would like to add to correct to what it was said before: the Abraham Accords in the region did not initiate something new. There was always a sort of longing amongst a lot of people in the Muslim world to reconnect with the Jewish world and to engage with Israel. Even though in many cases it was small or it was contained or was less public, but the Abraham Accords gave us a chance for more scalability of that kind of work, more visibility, because in the Middle East and North Africa we need the leadership to open and endorse this kind of work and allow this work to be more sustainable, more impactful and more scalable. So, in a way it is kind of a continuation of the history of the region, a return to the concept of *Convivencia*. We see this in the development of the Hebrew language: Hebrew went into its golden era because of the proximity with the Arabic language. In a sense, the Abraham Accords allow us to come back to a Middle East of pluralisms, to celebrate the multitude of identities in the region.

Omar Al Busaidy: Hi everyone. I am from the United Arab Emirates, specifically Dubai. I am an author, a Fulbright Scholar. I did my masters at Florida State in international affairs. I have always been an advocate for coexistence and tolerance. I got this first from my home, my parents, but also from the leadership of our country, and that is why I got involved with Sharaka, our organization ("sharaka" means "partnership" in Arabic). If you haven't been to the UAE yet, the UAE was founded in 1971 (next month we are celebrating 50 years), we are like 9 million people, out of which the UAE citizens are only about ten percent. When you have people from all over the world, with different cultures and religions – by the way, we always had also a Jewish community in the UAE – it was only naturally for me to celebrate the Abraham Accords when they were announced last year. And I think – I will second Chama here – what the Abraham Accords did was just to ignite that longing from the Muslim World and Arabs to really meet and finally connect with their Jewish cousins, literally. There were a lot of Israelis who traveled to the UAE for business. I used to actually receive them and speak to these delegations. The founders of Sharaka approached me and said: "*You are an Emirati who lives in the US, would you be interested in leading the organization in the US?*" So, I am now the CEO of Sharaka in the US. I love it. This delegation is the second coming to the US. We had a first delegation that went to New York, Boston and Atlanta. We spoke to many different communities there. They were very welcoming. Many were tearful when they heard our stories and the activities that Sharaka is organizing in the UAE: We celebrate in the UAE a lot of cultural events, like *Lag Baomer* [a Jewish festival 2000-years old] and *Iftar* [a Muslim celebration] during the month of Ramadan. We are here to tell this story, this new narrative that is taking place in the Middle East, because unfortunately the western media does not cover these events. We felt it was necessary for us to be present here and to tell this story and we hope that you will carry our message to other people as you hear our stories.

117

Dan Feferman: I am the Director of Global Affairs and Communications for Sharaka, based in Israel. I was born in the US, grew up in Indiana to an Israeli-American family, and I moved back to Israel in 2005. I spent close to a decade in the Israel Defense forces, in the national security world as a Middle East and national security policy analyst and adviser. Since then, I have been a research fellow at a Jerusalem-based think-tank where I focus on primarily on Jewish World issues, Israeli-Diaspora relations, trends in the Israeli society, trends in the American-Jewish society and, hopefully, in the next couple of months I will be publishing my second book on these matters. I lecture, I podcast and I consult on a variety of matters. The story of the Abraham Accords, the story of Sharaka, of what we are doing, is essentially my story. I guess that everyone of us has that story and this is why we are all now sitting here together. I have always been fascinated with the Middle East. Israel is, of course, part of the Middle East, but unfortunately because of the conflict we have been cut off. Even inside of Israel, as Lorena mentioned, we have close to a quarter of our country that is actually an Arab minority, an although we get along on a day-to-day basis it is hard to say that most Israeli Jews and most Israeli Arabs have close personal connections. Some do. It is getting better I think, but on a day-to-day level we don't, and because of the conflict and because of the region, we have been cut off from our neighbors, from our cousins. Most of you probably know this: more than half of the Israeli Jews have their origins in the Middle East. Half of my family came from Iraq, Iraqi Jews who had to flee in the ninety-fifties because of growing antisemitism and that story is not unique in Israel. So, the Arab and the middle eastern culture and the language and the food and the music are part of my growing up as they are for many Israelis, but we could never openly travel. I spent my college years studying the Middle East and studying Arabic, and then spent a decade in the military being engaged in the region in a very different way. I continued lecturing over the years and in those lectures, when I recently went back over my notes, I noticed a progression of developing regional trends and the growing signs of progress and closeness between Israel and the Gulf countries. One by one by one: a sports delegation, a public ministerial visit, an Arab government in the Gulf wishing Rosh Hashana, blessings to the Jewish people. One by one by one. When the Abraham Accords were announced, I was invited to join the group, I had helped founding the group, the UAE-Israel business council, and I was one of the first Israelis to visit the Gulf. I toured a little bit, but what I mostly did was meeting people, people I had networked on line with them for months already, getting to know them. And every single Emirati and not just Emirati, but Syrians, Palestinians, Egyptians, Iranians who live in the UAE, it was like we were long lost brothers and sisters, who just couldn't talk to each other for a long time, every conversation was immediately a deep connection, and I realized a couple of things: first of all, there is a new Middle East here for us, the Accords were a watershed moment in our modern history, in that the region the day before and the day after will not be the same. It lifted a Sand Curtain, so to speak (like the Iron Curtain), a Sand Curtain of legitimacy for these things that had been happening for the better part of the decade since the Arab Spring, of people realizing that they have been lied to, people realizing they have been radicalized, people realizing they have been divided in concrete for too long for cynical and political reasons. And through social media, and through access to the internet and through travels abroad, this groundswell of young, hopeful, educated people, who just wanted a better life for themselves said: *"Can this be the only way, can there be a better way?"*. And we need to be talking about these people in Israel. I saw a vision of the Middle East that is moderate, that is forward looking, that is pragmatic, that is open, that is tolerant. Everything that we were taught that the Arab world isn't. Everything that we were taught in Israel and in the West that the Muslim world isn't. And I saw women's rights, women's empowerment. And I came back to Israel and people couldn't believe the things that I was saying. Like Omar, I was interviewed in TV, and was writing in papers, I was acting on my own. And then Sharaka called and said: *"Would you like to join us?"* And I said, this is the opportunity of a lifetime to join these people to make sure that these governmental agreements are translated and expanded on the people-to-people level, and we need to grow this movement, we need to grow this circle, and that is what we are trying to do back in the Middle East, and this is the story we wanted to tell you today.

Don Gilbert: In your really impressive, thoughtful, comprehensible introduction you basically got my twelve questions out of the way and I can only talk about food and sports. But I will try: it feels like to some extent the Abraham Accords may be somewhat generational. Who wants to go first?

45:40 / 1:24:33

Chama Mechtaly: I will speak about Morocco and I will leave to my colleagues speak about Bahrain, Syria and the region. In the case of Morocco, the relationship between Israel and Morocco goes back to 1948. Morocco has always maintained relationships with Israel, sometimes more open, sometimes less so. Morocco had a liaison office in Tel Aviv through the nineties that was shut down in 2000 following the Intifada and pressure, because Morocco is part of the Arab League and still is. There was pressure following the Intifada to shut it down, the King had just stepped into power in 1999, so he was a young king under a lot of pressure to consolidate power. However, because the cultural and social ties and relationships are historical and extremely deep, even in the context of political differences and the freezing of the political relationships, the cultural and social relationships remained. This is due first of all because Israel counts a massive Moroccan Jewish community: one in nine Israelis is Moroccan on both sides and there are a lot of people that are mixed Moroccan and Ashkenazi. The second factor is that even after the departure of the biggest numbers of the Moroccan Jewish community, there remained traces and sacred spaces and cemeteries. Morocco is the only country in the region that has a Jewish Museum, so there was exposure in some ways to the Jewish history in the country. Of course, over the last few decades we have obviously suffered in a rise in the fundamentalist ideology that has restricted not just civil liberties and the consciousness over the history but also the extent to which people express that complexity and that story around the Moroccan Jewry. And specifically, within the last ten years, since the Arab Spring in 2011, we had three Islamist governments successively. I myself was censured for showcasing Jewish art in Casablanca and, repetitively, even before that, I would get invited to exhibit my paintings and then at the last minute I would be told there was no way to do that, again because the government had just no tolerance for representing that kind of pluralism. However, it is also strategic for the leadership of the country to also fight the forces of extremism, so there has been this calculated and strategic effort to counter extremism by highlighting the pluralism in the country and enforcing an agenda of interfaith dialog and tolerance. But the social fabric already exists to support that, and there is always civil society working in that direction and, even before the Abraham Accords, many activists were pro-normalization, went to Israel and came back to write about it in Arabic and to speak about it in the Moroccan language. Again, these stories would never make it into the US or the West, but they always existed. There is this deep feeling that part of understanding Moroccan history or North Africa history relies on understanding Jewish history. This is specifically common amongst the most educated or the most activist factions of the society. I will show you with a quick story about this: I was at an event with the Israeli ambassador last month in Morocco with civil society actors and activists and they said: *"Look, if you scratch the skin of a Moroccan, you will first find that they are indigenous. And if you do it a second time, you will find that they are Jewish"*. So, there is this deep consciousness of that history, that unfortunately because of the politics and the ideologies that were ruling and dictating what kind of policies took shape in the region, there was less openness about this recognition. And now, maybe I will pass the mic to Hayvi.

Hayvi Bouzo: I will be talking from a different angle. I was born in Damascus, Syria, which, as you know, is different from the political situation in North Africa. Iraq, Syria, Lebanon: these are countries that in the last decade there was there a complete domination by Iranian-backed militias, and the Iranian regime has basically spread a narrative that is very anti-Israel, very militant, that basically aims to the destruction of Israel. And this has also happened in Gaza with Hamas. This narrative has been brainwashing people and there is a propaganda machine in place for this purpose. However, people started seeing lately how these militias – backed by the Iranian regime – where slaughtering people, their own people. People began asking questions: *"Well. this is what you have been telling us, but this is what you were doing actually to us"*. So, there is that awakening, people started learning about the history that was hidden. About Israel's history in this region. For example, in the Koran, Israel is mentioned forty-three times. And Palestine is not even mentioned. There is a history, but Iran and the Iranian-backed militias do not want peace. So, yes, there are those questions, people are trying to learn, there is a generational change, but there are also these other factors that are playing a big role.

Omar Al Busaidy: The one thing that the UAE and Israel share the most is that both countries respect tradition but embrace modernism. The UAE from the very beginning has always been a place where they focus on economic development, prosperity, openness, cooperation, all of these different things that allowed for the leadership and its policies to identify strategic partners and allies to help them achieve the vision of the reality that we see today in the modern UAE. Now, having said that, we could not openly at that time announce that we had relations with Israel. The biggest cooperation between the UAE and Israel, for decades by the way, was in security: both countries face common threats. Their opportunities for progress were similar as well – as we see today especially when it comes to space exploration, climate change and agritech – so they have been talking to each other for many years, but it was always under the table. Sometimes it would be open, sometimes it would go away – as Chama said: you would see ministers coming to the UAE, attending a conference, etc., but then it would go away. What happened though, and what led finally to allowing the Abraham Accords to come into fruition is that the UAE said: "*You know what, let us do it smartly*". They established in 2016 something they called the *Ministry of Tolerance and Coexistence*. On the surface it did not make sense, because we were already being tolerant and in coexistence with everybody. And then – this reminds me what Chama was saying before regarding Morocco – they announced "*The Year of Tolerance*" and they invited the Pope to come to the UAE for the first time. And then, they announced something they called "*The UAE Moral Education*", where they started to educate children about accepting people from different backgrounds; and then you would see Israeli athletes coming to take part in competitions the UAE organized. And when they came, the Israeli national anthem would play. And you would see ministers of Israel attending conferences openly. And then, slowly but surely, the UAE was the first country to announce that they were going to sign the Abraham Accords. And this led

122

the way for Bahrain, Morocco and Sudan, and hopefully other Arab states and non-Arab states to join the Abraham Accords. So that is how, stage by stage, they got to get to the point where we are today.

Don Gilbert: Great, thank you. The next question is for the second half of the panel: Have the Abraham Accords unleashed something in the Middle East that is unstoppable, or could it be derailed? And let us start with Fatema.

Fatema Al Harbi: For me, to speak about the Bahrain situation, the change has been huge. It is not as much as the UAE but we started to see the change that the Abrahamic Accord has affected. We used to see Israel in a very negative way. Now even in the national media outlets, newspapers, we see Israel mentioned every day in a very positive way. And people are not used to it and I understand that it will take time for them to adjust to the new situation. We are having the flights, the direct flights from Bahrain to Israel twice a week. People have started asking how can they get visas, how can they get to Israel. So, a lot of new movements are happening in Bahrain. And, thankfully, it is happening between people to people. It is not on a governmental level only. So, this is the situation in Bahrain.

Lorena Khateeb: For me it is kind of a process, we can see how this change will look like in the next few years. People always ask me: *"Lorena, what do you do?"* I always mention that I work as a construction worker. I build bridges between people. I think that this is what we are doing in Sharaka, we are like preparing the ground for the people to get the idea, to get into this new path of peace and stability in the Middle East. People were raised like brainwashed, as Fatema said, they saw Israel as an enemy, as a place that you cannot go and visit and explore by yourself. I think that the peace agreements have opened a great opportunity for people from all the Arab world to go to Israel and explore Israel by themselves and to see the reality and to share it with their people. This is the change we are living now.

Dan Feferman: I think that all processes – if anything History teaches us – is that all processes are reversible. I think that History is not linear. Thomas Friedman writes that everything is marching towards Democracy. It turns out that History does not work that way. It turns out that everything is stoppable. It is sad to say. Good processes can be halted. But also, that means that bad processes can also be halted and good ones can be initiated. And I think that, you know – sorry for philosophizing here on stage – if this moment teaches us something is that we all can change History. Now in this case we needed the governments to step in here. I am an optimistic person by nature. I think this unleashed something that has a lot of momentum, but that means that we cannot just sit back and let it happen. That is why we, everyone, all of us here, need to be proactive in this to make sure that it does not just stop. The only way to fight extremism, negativity, is by giving an alternative, a positive alternative. Show that cooperation is in everyone's interest and to drown out the noise of extremism. You do not do it by extremism, but by moderation and positivity. So, it was a huge step but we cannot sit back, we have to be incredible proactive about this, and keep spreading it, this is what we and everyone has to keep doing, in order to be sure that the momentum snowballs, it just keeps getting bigger and bigger and more people on board. Like a train, everyone should get into this train.

Don Gilbert: Great answers. I am going to ask one more question before the audience has a chance to ask. I am just going to ask Lorena and Omar one more question. My question in short is: *What about the Palestinians?* Hamas, no surprise, came out saying "*you are traitors*" and the Palestinian Authority was not that far behind. How that this affect you? What about the Palestinians? How do they fit into this? What are the opportunities that are there for them? Or, are they being ostracized?

Omar Al Busaidy: It is a great question. First of all, it is very important to note, number one, that there are hundreds of thousands of Palestinians living in the UAE and continue to do so. Number two, it is true that when the UAE signed the Abraham Accords, the Palestinian Authority removed its ambassador from the UAE – who by the way got its salary from the UAE government – and they also called for an emergency meeting of the Arab League to denounce the Abraham Accords. But the Arab League told the Palestinian Authority that the UAE is a sovereign state and they have the right to take the decisions that they see as necessary for its own interest. In spite of the fact that this has happened, the UAE did not do anything to disrupt the lives of the Palestinians living in the UAE. Second, during this pandemic the UAE continues to send aid to the Palestinians both in the West Bank and in the Gaza strip. In fact, we sent the Russian vaccine, Sputnik, and Hamas actually came on in the media and thanked the Russian government for it, although we were the ones who sent it. It is fine for us as long as the people are going to be OK, are going to be healthy, alive and well. That is what matters. Getting the recognition does not really matter for us. If you go on the news right now, you will see that the UAE government is actively working on rebuilding the schools and hospitals in Gaza after the conflict that happened earlier this year. We are still supporting them. If you come right now in the UAE, we have a massive event, the World Fair, called Expo, in Dubai, and when you come there you will see that we have 190 countries represented, and you see the State of Israel and you see the State of Palestine. We always have been supportive of the Palestinians. Just because this conflict in the region and this conflict between the Palestinians and Israelis, it does not mean that we cannot engage with Israel. We have relations with many other countries that we disapprove of some of their policies but we are still engaged with them. In international relations, in international norms, there are rules of engagement and this is what the UAE believes in and will work with and, at the end of the day, when the Palestinian Authority decides to come and have a conversation with us our arms are open, we will have a discussion with them and, hopefully, if they want us to have a sit on the table – instead of always bringing the US to try to solve the Middle East problems –we will be very active in that cause. That is my take on the UAE and the Palestinians.

Lorena Khateeb: I think that every single person, not only the Palestinian people, will benefit from these peace agreements. We all have to remember that in the Palestinian-Israeli conflict there are two sides, there is the Israeli side and there is the Palestinian side, but the media is always trying to cover only the Palestinian narrative. Israel has given the Palestinian Authority and its people hundreds of opportunities for peace and they have ignored it. I think that the first step is by recognizing Israel as an independent state. This peace treaty will help Israelis to connect more and more with the Palestinian people. It all begins with dialog. The UAE has done a huge step by the announcement of the peace agreements and I think that it helps all the region, because we saw Bahrain join the peace agreements and then Sudan and Morocco, and hopefully more countries will join us. We have tried the path of conflict and war for many years. We have to try a new way, a new path of stability with the whole region.

Dan Feferman: May I add a few comments? It is burning on me. The regional strategy that the Palestinians tried, and for a while the Arab world, was pressure Israel, boycott Israel, isolate Israel. First through war that failed, and then through terror that did not succeed. Economic boycotts, diplomatic boycotts. It did not work. It did not work for the Palestinians and the region realizes it: The UAE, Bahrain, Morocco. They realized that is not even helping the Palestinians. If it would – forget that I am an Israeli – go for it. If that is what gets to your goal, do it. It did not work and it only made things worse because, as an Israeli, I can say it made us more closed off. I still remember the Oslo Accords. I grew up in a generation that was very hopeful that peace was so close – and we missed it. But today's generation of kids? They only know of the Intifada, of the rockets, of Hamas, of suicide bombings and stabbings. That is the only Arab world they know. I remember a sliver of the Palestinian world where we could have been friends. I still remember that. And the further you get away from that, the more and more the "*Arab*" image – again, remember because we did not have a relationship with the broader Arab world, we only had a relation with the Palestinians – was a negative one, was seen as scary: they hated us. I truly hope, I think that we all truly hope, that if this [the Abraham Accords] can humanize the Arab world, the Muslim world, for the Israelis, and vice versa, that eventually the Palestinians will realize that it will warm the entire atmosphere around us, it will eventually bring us come together. It also brings actors – like the UAE, Bahrain and Morocco – to the table as positive influences on Israel and on the Palestinians, to bring them together. I don't think the Palestinians were ignored, but I do think that it was about time that someone would said enough holding everyone hostage to something that is just not working. Let us try a new path and – from the Arab world perspective – I think the intent will lead to a Palestinian something, one day in peace, certainly.

Don Gilbert: I hope that you are right. OK. We have time now for a few questions from the audience.

[**A member of the audience**]: Thank you. My name is Tarah. I was born in Iran and I am a US citizen, we have been in this country for forty-four years. I just came with a friend to this program. I wasn't really much aware of the Abraham Accords and I just looked it up: It says "a joint statement between the State of Israel, the United Arab Emirates and the United States of America", and then it says a little further down that it was signed by the Emirati foreign minister, the Bahraini foreign minister, the Israeli Prime Minister and the US President Donald Trump, whose position towards Iran is very well known. I do not have any sympathies towards the regime of Iran, but as someone who was born in Iran, when I hear from the podium that when you talk about Iran – which is a nation with 7,000 years of history – and a huge history of Judaism, I really feel a little surprised that Iran is not mentioned, which is similar to the question you [Dan Gilbert] had [about the Palestinians]. I know that country, I was raised in Iran: there was nothing against Judaism, never. With these guys I am with – in the group "*Salam, Shalom*" – as we were children, we played on a court "*Hava Nagila*" [a Jewish-Israeli song] and recently for the first time after many, many years I started looking up and finding what did that mean what we constantly sang. I was actually raised in a family that was not religious, but from a Muslim background. So, Iran is not just the Iranian government. It is an absolute huge mistake to think that Iranian people are anti-Jewish. And that has to be said, when you say "Iran, and Hamas and Hezbollah". That is just not Iran.

1:14:51 / 1:24:33

Hayvi Bouzo: Can I respond to this? Your point is so important. Thank you so much for this. I used to live in Los Angeles, and a lot of my friends were Iranians. Many of them were Jewish Iranians and they were clothed in Persian clothes, and they were very proud of their Persian identity, and their community was Jewish and Muslim together. And I know so many Iranians until today, as a journalist covering the Middle East. Personally, all of the people that I know are anti-Iranian regime, which is what I am talking about today, in terms of who is sponsoring these Iranian militias. By the way, there are so many videos on-line that I know, where the Iranian regime puts American and Israeli flags on the floor for people to step on when they are walking down the streets. You see *none* of the people do. They all go around and, in traffic, on the entrance to colleges and universities, in the streets. Nobody would step on the American and Israeli flags, because they know, actually they know more than anybody in the region, that Israel is an allay, is not an enemy. There is a person that I know in D.C., who actually created something called "The Cyrus Accords" [*], and he brought a delegation of Iranians who want peace with Israel and they actually went and visited Israel so that they could be like complement to the Abraham Accords. So, the "Cyrus Accords" is happening: so many Iranians have expressed that this is what they want. Like you said, there is a very long history, there is a lot of historic alliance between the Jewish people and the Persians, before the Iranian revolution took over. So, yes, I agree completely with you.

[*] Note: Cyrus was a king of Persia in ancient times, who is revered by the Jews. In 538 BCE Cyrus granted Jewish exiles the right to return to Israel and rebuild their Temple in Jerusalem.

Don Gilbert: We have time for one more question.

[A member of the audience]: Shalom. Good to see you. As a rabbi, I was wondering if this is an initiative of global, young, cool, secular, generational initiative. I know, I am just being provocative. Or, is there a religious component to this? I am asking, we are sitting in a synagogue, we all share this. You know, we put this aside some times, but a lot of the conflict in the Middle East is religious. It has to do with religious conflict. So, I was wondering how you see the religious narratives and practices support, get in the way, help, resist – whatever you think – this initiative. Thank you.

Hayvi Bouzo: I was going to mention this briefly. I had a couple of shows where I had a rabbi, a sheikh and a priest, because as you say, the religious component is very important. People are very curious. We were just talking before coming to this round table about an initiative that *Sharaka* wants to make and that I am going to cover as a journalist, about having these dialogs, because they are so important. People do not know about Judaism, for example. The vast majority of people want to learn, and the more you know, the more you feel the closeness and the similarities, and the common history.

Dan Feferman: I will share a short story. In my first trip to Dubai, I went to the UAE to the Arab's world first kosher restaurant, with three traditional Muslim Arab friends in traditional dress. And I am sitting there, the only Jew in this Muslim table, and we spoke all night, exchanging stories, learning things from each other religions, and traditions and history. And the evening started with me going to do "*Netilat Yadaim*", to wash our hands, as we traditionally do ceremoniously before we eat our bread. And my friend got up to do it with me: "*I want to do it with you*", he said. We sat down, the three of us and we said "*Ha'motsi*" together in the heart of the Arab world ["*Ha'motsi*": Hebrew word meaning "*who brings forth*". First word of the traditional ritual prayer "*Who brings forth bread from the Earth*".] And then we spoke until three in the morning, exchanging those kinds of stories. This will be one of our [*Sharaka*] next initiatives we are launching, for people on-line to be able to do this. Absolutely.

Don Gilbert: I just wanted to thank you all. I have to say: it is so up-lifting, it is so refreshing to hear what you have to say. It is kind of nurturing for the soul. I think that a lot of what you said, frankly, is a surprise to many in the American Jewish community. So, I hope you go and talk to a lot of more, more people. And when you are really brave, go to college campuses.

Lesson 7

"Arafat was also trying to wiggle out of giving up the right of return. He knew he had to but was afraid of the criticism he would get. I reminded him that Israel had promised to take some of the refugees from Lebanon whose families had lived in what was now northern Israel for hundreds of years, but that no Israeli leader would ever let in so many Palestinians that the Jewish character of the state could be threatened in a few decades by the higher Palestinian birthrate. There were not going to be two majority-Arab states in the Holy Land."

President Bill Clinton, recounting his conversations with the Palestinian leader Yasser Arafat in Camp David, year 2000 (From his autobiography "My Life", 2005)

"The issue of the refugees must be resolved. There are refugees and they should return. I am a refugee. I am a Palestinian refugee. I want to return to my town. I cannot live even in Paris or New York. I won't have it. I want Safed [a city in Israel]. It is such a small town. I want it."

Mahmoud Abbas, the Palestinian President, in his address at the UN, on **May 15, 2023**

Note

Every book represents solely the views of its author. Nevertheless, I tried so far to largely represent the views of many or, at least, the views of a significant number of Jews, and non-Jews.

Lesson 7 differs from the previous lessons in that I do not claim to represent the views of many. Definitely: it is my view.

It helps stating my personal view in that the main purpose of this lesson is not to describe the past as it happened (even this is not exact science: history is also subjected to interpretations, some more faithful to the events than others), but to present a vision of the future, although still based on the experiences of the past and the conditions of the present.

It is time to move on

Introduction

"On May 15, 2023, the Palestinian President Mahmoud Abbas, in a speech at the UN commemorating the Nakba, urged the United Nations to suspend Israel's membership unless it implements resolutions establishing separate Jewish and Arab states and the return of Palestinian refugees.

The [UN] General Assembly, which had 57 member nations in 1947, approved the resolution dividing Palestine by a vote of 33-13 with 10 abstentions. The Jewish side accepted the U.N. partition plan and after the British mandate expired in 1948, Israel declared its independence. The Arabs rejected the plan and neighboring Arab countries launched a war against the Jewish state.

The Nakba commemorates the estimated 700,000 Palestinians who fled or were forced from their homes in [the] 1948 [war].

The fate of these refugees and their descendants – estimated at over 5 million across the Middle East – remains a major disputed issue in the Arab-Israeli conflict. Israel rejects demands for a mass return of refugees to long-lost homes, saying it would threaten the country's Jewish character."

(Reported by Edith M. Lederer, Associated Press, published in the *Washington Post* newspaper, on May 15, 2023)

Two days later, I published the following article in the "*Times of Israel*" newspaper:

Abbas' speech at the UN: Stuck in his past

(Published in the "Times of Israel" newspaper, May 17, 2023)

Abbas' speech at the UN is old and repeated stuff. Jews should return to their "dhimmi" minority status they had in the Arab world in two stages. First stage: return to the 1949 armistice lines (through the implementation of the "2-state solution"); second stage: return of the Jews to their status prior to 1948 as a "tolerated" minority also in Israel proper (through the demand for the "return of the Palestinian refugees" to Israel). This is the solution of the Arab-Israeli conflict in the eyes of the Palestinians in the West Bank.

Hamas proposes the return of the Jews to their "dhimmi" status directly in one-step, by eliminating the State of Israel through violent means. As they state at the beginning of their 1988 Covenant: *"Islam will obliterate Israel, as it obliterated others before it"* and *"initiatives, and so-called peaceful solutions are in contradiction to the principles of the Islamic Resistance Movement ... a waste of time and vain endeavors."* This is the solution of the Arab-Israeli conflict in the eyes of the Palestinians in Gaza.

Both the Palestinians in the West Bank and in Gaza aim to achieve the same goal: In their view, the land between the Jordan River and the Mediterranean Sea was and will be Arab land, forever. Jews interested in living there should accept their status as "dhimmis", the status of a submissive "tolerated" minority. Jews who will not accept their "dhimmi" status, will be dealt with according to the Islamic principles that hold in Arab lands, read: expelled or killed.

A bit of recent History

Camp David (2000) failed because the Palestinians would not give up their "right to return", after Israel had accepted the "Clinton parameters" for a 2-state solution.

The 2005 disengagement from Gaza was wrong: Recapturing now Gaza will be wrong. I do not blame the Israeli government for what it did in 2005. The intentions were good: Gaza at that time posed a smaller security risk and the idea of leaving Gaza to the Palestinians to give peace a chance, praying that they would do the right thing and develop Gaza for the benefit of the Palestinians, was philosophically noble – but politically shortsighted, showing a lack of understanding of the profound rejectionism and irredentism Palestinians are imbued with.

The Oslo Accords in 1994 were wrong. Ignoring the United Nations Security Council (UNSC) resolution 242 and Jordan, and embracing the Palestine Liberation Organization (PLO), showed an unusual level of naivety. What was the Israeli government thinking when they colluded with the PLO and bypassed Jordan?

Who was the PLO? The Palestine Liberation Organization had been founded in 1964, when the West Bank was under Jordanian rule and Gaza under Egypt rule. Its charter clearly said that they intended to eliminate Israel and return the situation in the region between the [Jordan] River and the [Mediterranean] Sea into what it was – not in 1949 – but in 1917, expulsing or killing the Jews and returning the Palestinians to Tel-Aviv, Haifa and Beer Sheva. The PLO had repeatedly shown its stripes: in Jordan it tried to bring the Hashemite Kingdom of Jordan down during the bloody Black September insurrection in 1970. Then, moving to Lebanon in the 1970s, the PLO managed to transform a beacon of peace and development in the Arab world into ruins, from which that country never recovered. With this *Resume* of "country building" in front of its eyes, the government of Israel decided to bypass Jordan and the UNSC 242, and make the PLO its partner in peace.

Nothing came out of the Oslo Accords, except for three Nobel Peace prizes bequeathed to Arafat, Rabin and Peres.

My 2-cents about how to solve the Arab-Israeli conflict

Israel must return to the UNSC Resolution 242 and negotiate with Jordan on a solution to the conflict. (For more details: see the Appendix to this chapter.) Gaza and the West Bank should be demilitarized and reincorporated as part of Jordan, perhaps the West Bank first and Gaza sometime later. As suggested elsewhere, Jordan will change its name to reflect this territorial union (the name Hashemite Kingdom of Palestine has lately been suggested), and an internationally recognized border between Israel and the Hashemite Kingdom of Palestine will be established to recognize the new reality.

An international aid program – similar to the Marshall Plan for Europe after World War II – should be established, as part of the solution to the Arab-Israeli conflict, to develop the economy of Jordan and integrate the Palestinians in the expanded Hashemite Kingdom of Palestine.

A similar proposition has been heard lately from circles close to the Saudi Royal family. I refer people to the article by Ali Shihabi, a close confident of Crown Prince Mohammed Bin Salman, in the Saudi Royal Family-owned news outlet "Al-Arabiya News", from last June 8, 2022:

https://english.alarabiya.net/in-translation/2022/06/08/The-Hashemite-Kingdom-of-Palestine

Quoting Ali Shihabi: *"The Palestinian problem can only be solved today if it is redefined. The most logical vehicle for this redefinition and hence for the solution to the Palestine problem is the kingdom of Jordan. Over the last seventy-five years, Jordan has developed into a relatively well-governed state, although the impact of regional political turmoil has caused it to fail economically and become heavily reliant on foreign aid for its survival. It is this Jordanian governance infrastructure that needs to be captured and put to productive use in integrating the millions of Palestinians and Jordanians into a modern, reasonably well-functioning state that would, in an era of real peace and economic integration with Jordan's neighbors, have a much higher chance of growth and prosperity.*

This proposed enlarged kingdom would include present-day Jordan, Gaza, and the West Bank (areas populated by Palestinians attached in a contiguous manner and physically connected to Jordan, i.e., not broken up into islands). Israeli arguments as to the need to retain the Jordan Valley become moot since the valley will now be controlled by a Jordanian government with a reliable record of maintaining peace with Israel. The convenient argument that Israel has no "peace partner" will now also be eliminated.

Jerusalem, despite the fact that neither Arabs nor Muslims have a hope of dislodging Israel from it, is, given its symbolism, a key bargaining chip in Palestinian hands. The formal relinquishment of any claims to Jerusalem (with an appropriate arrangement for the holy places) can be an important concession used to secure the foregoing terms. The Palestinians, after all, are the only party who can do this and, hence, completely legitimize Israel in the eyes of the region and the world."

[End of excerpts from Ali Shihabi's article]

I do not say that the return to the UNSC 242 and to the Jordanian track would be easy and accepted immediately by the world: it might take a long time for this proposal to sink in the minds of the people in the region and in the western world, and be implemented. But this vision should be clearly and explicitly adopted by Israel early on, in order to concentrate its limited human resources on the principal objective: *A Jewish and Democratic state, living in secure and recognized international borders.*

Time to move on: The Hashemite Kingdom of Palestine

(Published in the "Times of Israel" newspaper, June 4, 2023)

Year 1967:

On May 18, 1967, the United Arab Republic (then a union of Egypt and Syria) requested the United Nations to withdraw the UN forces from the Sinai Peninsula and the Gaza Strip, stationed there to maintain a quiet border with Israel. The UN protested but it complied with the request.

Four days later, on May 22, 1967, Egypt closed the Straits of Tiran to navigation to and from Israel. At that time around 90% of the vital oil imports to Israel (from Iran) passed through the Straits of Tiran. This triggered, two weeks later, the June 1967 war. The war pitted Egypt, Syria and Jordan against Israel, and its effects are felt till today. The main results of this war were: Egypt lost the Sinai Peninsula and the Gaza Strip, Syria lost the Golan Heights, and Jordan lost the West Bank.

In November 1967 the United Nations Security Council adopted the resolution 242 that set the principles for the resolution of the conflict between Israel and the Arab countries.

Year 2000:

President Bill Clinton gave a pointedly summary of the negotiations between the Israeli and Palestinian teams held during July-December 2000, hosted by the US in Camp David:

"Arafat was also trying to wiggle out of giving up the right of return … I reminded him that there were not going to be two majority-Arab states in the Holy Land…Arafat's rejection of my proposal [the 'Clinton parameters'] after Barak accepted it was an error of historic proportions." [President Bill Clinton, recounting his conversations with the Palestinian leader Yasser Arafat in Camp David, in year 2000 (From his autobiographic book "My Life", 2005)]

The 2-state approach

The 2-state approach has been pursued by all stripes of the political spectrum of Israel: by the **leftist Labor** (prime minister Ehud Barak: in Camp David, 2000, who accepted president Clinton's parameters for the resolution of the conflict with the Palestinians), by the **rightist Likud** (prime minister Ariel Sharon: who – in a unilateral move – removed all the Jews from Gaza in 2005, and left the strip to the Palestinian Authority), and by the **centrist Kadima** (prime minister Ehud Olmert, who made further concessions to the Palestinians in matters related to Jerusalem, in 2008). All these efforts failed to produce any results.

It is time to move on.

Year 2023:

Israel must return to the UNSC Resolution 242 and negotiate with Jordan an end to the conflict. The main items to resolve the conflict are its territorial and refugee aspects.

The territorial aspect: Gaza and the West Bank should be demilitarized and reincorporated as part of Jordan, perhaps the West Bank first and Gaza sometime later.

The demilitarization of the West Bank

Figure 7.1: Israel, the West Bank and Gaza. (Map source: the US State Department)

Notice the width of the state of Israel in its heavily populated area along the Mediterranean Sea: It is only about 10-20 miles. A demilitarized West Bank would provide a minimum safeguard to Israel against a sudden deterioration of the political situation in the West Bank and a consequent military aggression that could threaten its heavily populated center and "cut" Israel into two halves at its thin waist. A demilitarized West Bank, as part of Jordan, will not hurt the national feelings of sovereignty of anyone: It already works fine for many years with Egypt's Sinai.

As suggested elsewhere, Jordan will change its name to reflect this territorial union (the name *"Hashemite Kingdom of Palestine"* has lately been suggested in an article published in the Saudi Royal Family-owned news outlet "Al-Arabiya News", last June 8, 2022), and an internationally recognized border between Israel and the Hashemite Kingdom of Palestine will be established to recognize the new reality.

The refugee aspect: An international aid program – similar to the Marshall Plan for Europe after World War II – should be established, as part of the solution to the Arab-Israeli conflict, to develop the economy of Jordan and integrate the Palestinians in the expanded Hashemite Kingdom of Palestine.

I do not say that the return to the UNSC 242 and to the Jordanian track would be easy and accepted immediately by the world: it might take some time for this proposal to sink in the minds of the people in the region and in the western world, and be implemented. But this vision should be clearly and explicitly adopted by Israel early on: It is in Israel's best interests, in order to concentrate its limited human resources on the principal objective: *A Jewish and Democratic state, living in secure and recognized international borders.*

No one will be forced to leave his/her home

After a recognized international border between Israel and the Hashemite Kingdom of Palestine will be established, replacing the armistice (cease-fire) lines of 1949, some small Jewish towns, presently in the West Bank, might appear within the Hashemite Kingdom of Palestine international borders. Similarly, some small Arab towns, presently in the West Bank, might appear within the international border of Israel. The same might happen with some small Arab towns presently within Israel's 1949 armistice borders: they might appear within the Hashemite Kingdom of Palestine international borders. No one will be forced to leave his/her home, and the individual civil rights of these people will be respected. This will include their rights to keep their ties with their fellow citizens on the other side of the international border. This will also include their right to hold dual-citizenship.

The Hashemite Kingdom of Palestine

The Hashemite Kingdom of Palestine will include the present Kingdom of Jordan, the West Bank and the Gaza Strip.

The West Bank: A geographic perspective

The map below shows the relative size of Jordan and the West Bank. Jordan is comparable in size to the state of Indiana. The West Bank is around only 6% of the area of Jordan, and is comparable in size to the state of Delaware.

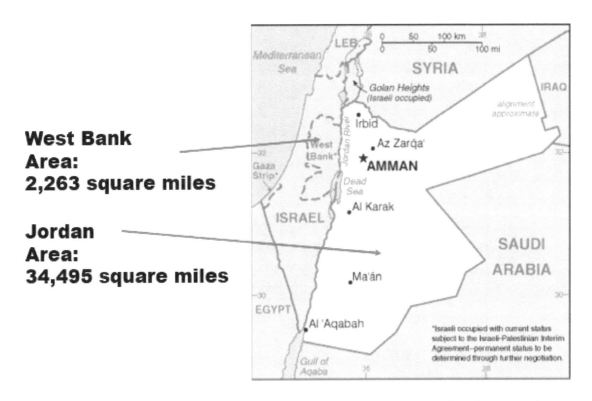

West Bank
Area:
2,263 square miles

Jordan
Area:
34,495 square miles

Figure 7.2: Jordan and the West Bank. (Map source: Central Intelligence Agency, USA)

The Gaza Strip: An economic perspective

The area of the Gaza Strip is only 140 square miles, with a population of about 2 million people. An underground tunnel joining Gaza to the West Bank (similar in length to the undersea channel between the UK islands and Europe, but easier to build and maintain) will put an end to the isolation of the Gaza territory, allowing for a free movement of people and goods. The economy of Gaza will now be sustainable: a port, a system of desalinization plants and tourism. For Jordan it means direct access to the Mediterranean Sea, and an underground aqueduct will provide a long-term solution to access to potable water to the Jordanian population: Jordan is presently practically a landlocked country with very limited water resources. For comparison: Israel desalinates 75% of its drinking water from the Mediterranean Sea. The aqueduct can also provide an ecologically-sound solution for the dying Dead Sea.

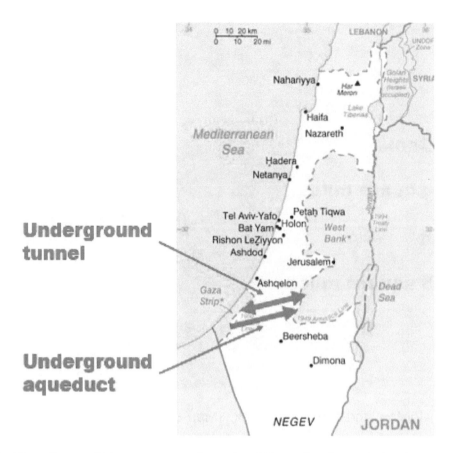

Figure 7.3: The Gaza Strip connected to the West Bank and Jordan through an underground tunnel and aqueduct. (Map source: The US State Department)

The map above shows the Gaza strip joined to the West Bank and Jordan through an underground tunnel (for the free movement of people and goods) and an underground aqueduct (to provide desalinized water to the West Bank and Jordan.)

The Gaza Strip: A timeline

The political future of Gaza will have to be postponed to a later time: it will have to be demilitarized, but, as long as the Ayatollahs remain in power in Iran, the stalemate in Gaza will persist. However, the reunification of the West Bank with Jordan could proceed to completion without having to "consult" Hamas, that is, without giving to Hamas a veto power, and let this process begin with the West Bank first.

-

It is time to move on.

Appendix

7.1 The 2-state approach: a fruitless detour from the 242

(Published in the "Jerusalem Post" newspaper, July 14, 2015)

The most important political outcome of the 1967 Israeli-Arab war was the 242 UNSC resolution outlining the parameters for a comprehensive and lasting solution of the Israeli-Arab conflict. It is worth reminding this in light of the present push by France for a UNSC resolution that would become a new framework for negotiations based on the 2-state approach.

What makes France so confident that it has the key on how to solve the Israeli-Arab conflict? Looking at the mess France created in Libya does not instill too much confidence in its wisdom: France's disgraceful military intervention toppled a regime that did not pose any threat to any neighbor, had renounced and dismantled its development of nuclear weapons and had fought Al-Qaeda sympathizers within its borders. France heralded it was bringing freedom and justice to Libya, but it left instead that country in complete shambles and ripe for extremist groups to take root in it and spread from there to other countries.

Politicians in the West, especially in Europe, love to criticize Netanyahu, seeing him and his policies as the main obstacle towards achieving the resolution of the Israeli-Palestinian conflict. They choose to ignore the fact that for the last twenty years the 2-state approach has been pursued by all stripes of the political spectrum of Israel - from left to right, from Ehud Barak to Ariel Sharon, from Olmert to Netanyahu - and failed to produce the hoped-for outcome. One can begin wondering about the sanity of trying again and again an approach that was already tried multiple times and failed to produce any tangible results. Is there an alternative to the failed 2-state approach in the middle of the upheaval going through the whole Middle East? *Yes, there is: the 1967 242 UNSC resolution.*

The implementation of the 242 got a good start with the Egypt-Israel peace treaty signed in 1979. The next step was expected to be a peace treaty with Jordan. However, in a surprise move, Israel and the Palestinian Liberation Organization signed in 1993 the Oslo Accords, bypassing Jordan. This temerarious approach (nowadays called the "2-state solution") enjoyed a short-lived Golden Age in the late nineties: three Nobel Peace prizes were awarded. However, it soon hit its first reality check when in 2000 the PLO rejected the peace proposal presented by President Clinton. Since then, it took a steep downturn from which it never recovered. The PLO launched an Intifada with suicide missions coming one after another from the West Bank and terminating in the Tel Aviv and Jerusalem streets. Hundreds of Israelis were murdered and thousands injured.

An effort to revive the moribund Oslo approach was taken by Israel in 2005, when – in a unilateral and dramatic move - it dismantled all the Jewish settlements in Gaza and left the strip to the PLO. The hope was that if the PLO could show that it could successfully govern the Gaza strip (that posed a smaller security risk to Israel), favor economic development and promote peaceful relationships with Israel, this model could later be tried on a larger scale in the West Bank. None of this happened: the PLO was not built for this challenge. Since 2007, after the violent takeover of the Gaza strip by Hamas, Gaza has been one more intractable issue for the proponents of the 2-state solution.

What would happen if Israel gives the control of the West Bank to the PLO, as envisioned in the 2-state approach? We will watch a second takeover by Hamas. The only reason that Abbas is still in charge of the West Bank today is because he has the backing of the Israel Defense Forces that keep Hamas in check. Tel-Aviv, Jerusalem and Ben-Gurion's airport are only a few miles away from the West Bank: Israel does not have the luxury to embark in a second Gaza-type experiment with the PLO.

The Oslo accords were an audacious attempt by Israel to solve the Israeli-Arab conflict. It will take political courage to recognize that this approach was a mistake and led to a dead end. Is there a sensible way out of this stalemate in the middle of the Arab Winter? Yes, there is: the 242 UNSC resolution.

Most Israelis - from left to right, secular and religious – are in favor of the partition of the land between the Mediterranean Sea and the Jordan River because they want to preserve the identity of a Jewish state. "Jewish" because they are proud of their roots in this land and of the contribution of the Jewish people to the human civilization in the arts and sciences, religion and philosophy, through History and they want to continue with this legacy and excel also in the future.

What is the main drive of the Palestinian struggle? It does not seem to be a state for a stateless people, living in peace with its neighbors. If this were the drive, it could have been reached long ago and in much more favorable circumstances. President Abbas' declaration, in his latest visit to Jordan, describing Jordanian and Palestinians Arabs as "one people living in two states" should not be ignored nor dismissed lightly.

Is there a path to return to the 242 approach? Yes: work now towards the reunification of the West Bank with Jordan. This approach has a much stronger chance of success: There are already peace treaties with Egypt and Jordan that have withstood the test of time. Palestinians in the West Bank have rich historical and family ties with Jordan. Half of the Jordanian population today is of Palestinian origin and they are fully integrated in the Jordanian society. Even the Queen of Jordan is Palestinian! Jordan has already a special official status in Jerusalem's holy Muslim sites. A demilitarized West Bank, as part of Jordan, will not hurt the national feelings of sovereignty of anyone: It already works fine for many years with Egypt's Sinai. Jordan has a stable and reliable regime that the Israelis trust. A "Marshall plan" should be implemented to help Jordan reintegrate the West Bank: This economic investment will ensure that Jordan remains a strong ally of the US for many years to come and help shield Israel and Jordan from the upheaval, instability and wars ravaging the Middle East.

What about the Gaza strip? Gaza could wait for a later time. The reunification of the West Bank with Jordan could proceed to completion without having to "consult" Hamas. In the meantime, a tight military embargo should be kept on Gaza, allowing at the same time commercial relations between the Gaza strip and the rest of the world. If Hamas wants to continue firing its missiles at Israeli towns and cities – Israel should hit back with full force. At some time, the Gaza people will get tired of Hamas, lose their fears and overthrow this regime. Gaza could flourish as an independent state, like Monaco or Singapore, or strive to join Egypt or Jordan. In all cases Gaza should be fully demilitarized. There is nothing that stands between the people of Gaza and a better future for their children, except for their present destructive approach towards Israel.

***

Lexicon and Notes

Ehud Barak: Leader of the **leftist** Labor Party. Served as Prime Minister from 1999 to 2001. During his term in office, he conducted the negotiations with the Palestinians in Camp David and accepted the "parameters" proposed by President Clinton to solve the Palestinian-Israeli conflict.

Ariel Sharon: Leader of the **rightist** Likud Party. Served as Primer Minister from 2001 to 2006. He led the 2005 unilateral "disengagement" from the Gaza Strip, during which all the Jewish settlements in Gaza were evacuated and all the Israeli troops withdrew from the Gaza Strip, leaving Gaza to the Palestinian Authority.

Ehud Olmert: Leader of the **centrist** Kadima party. Served as Prime Minister from 2006 to 2009. During his term he made an undisclosed offer to Mahmoud Abbas, then the leader of the Palestinians, for the termination of the Palestine-Israel conflict. Olmert's proposal included further Israeli concessions beyond the ones the Israelis accepted in Camp David in 2000, revolving mainly about the status of Jerusalem. For reasons unclear to the public, Abbas did not respond to Olmert's offer, and there was no follow-up. From what leaked to the press, the main sticking point was again the "right of return" of the Palestinians.

Benjamin Netanyahu: Leader of the **rightist** Likud Party. Served as Prime Minister from 1996 to 1999, when it was defeated by Ehud Barak. In 2009 Netanyahu was reelected as Prime Minister, succeeding Ehud Olmert. At the time the above article was published, in 2015, he still served as Prime Minister.

7.2 What can be learned from Afghanistan

(Published in the "Times of Israel" newspaper, August 22, 2021)

The recent debacle of the US in Afghanistan should put an end to the naïve idea that the Palestinian Authority (PA) in the West Bank – with some military aid to oppose a Hamas takeover, a shallow façade of democratic institutions and declarations of *"unwavering support"* from the US – will stand on its own, be strong enough, and willing to make peace with the Jewish State.

Hamas has the will to fight and will prevail in the West Bank, if left in the hands of the PA: Hamas has a much simpler effective platform vis-à-vis Israel, easily understandable to the masses at the gut and emotional level. And it is expeditious in its way to eliminate the political opposition of the PA, as it did in Gaza in 2007: murders, throwing people from the roofs and incarcerations.

The difference between Hamas in Gaza and the Palestinian Authority (PA) in the West Bank is only in the means but not in the end result. Hamas has a clear objective and a path to reach it (proven quite successful in the past thousand years): the land from the Jordan River to the Mediterranean Sea belongs to the Umma (Islamic communities) and can never be relinquished and the way to eliminate Israel is by force. The PA – having discarded the violent path after the unsuccessful Intifadas launched in 1987 and 2000 – intends to achieve the dissolution of the State of Israel by *"non-violent"* means: all the peace initiatives between the PA and Israel failed so far because of the refusal of the PA to renounce to the *"right of return"* of *millions* of Palestinians to Israel proper and to a formal declaration of an *"end to the conflict"*.

A mini-state in the West Bank, 40 miles wide by 55 miles long, would be overrun by Hamas and the Islamic Jihad. The only realistic way forward is to return to the original 242 UNSC resolution, with the West Bank as part of Jordan and demilitarized. A similar scheme has been successfully implemented between Egypt and Israel in the Sinai Peninsula.

The political future of Gaza will have to be postponed to a later time: it will have to be demilitarized, but as long as the Ayatollahs remain in power in Iran, the stalemate in Gaza will persist.

Lesson 8

October 7th 2023 – the massacre of Jews in Israel

On October 7th, 2023, the rulers of Gaza launched a surprise attack against Israel ("surprise" to those who did not care to read or believe Hamas' 1988 Covenant [see Appendix 7.1]). It was an unprovoked attack, on Saturday early morning, during the Jewish holiday of Sukkot. In a few hours – and while barrages of rockets reached the Israeli cities of Ashkelon, Ashdod and even as far as Tel-Aviv – several thousands of Hamas and Islamic Jihad terrorists breached the 1950 armistice border between Gaza and Israel, entered Israeli towns and butchered its citizens, in a rampage that surpassed the scenes of atrocities perpetuated by ISIS in Iraq. More than 1,200 civilians were killed and about 200 were taken hostages and dragged to Gaza – young children, women, and Holocaust survivors between them.

Since the year 2006, when Hamas won the elections in Gaza, this pattern of confrontations with Israel had been repeated every few years. What was new now was the territorial invasion into the southern Israeli towns and the horrendous premeditated butchery that followed. Hamas and Iran had seized the opportunity presented by the sharp internal political divisions within Israel that had diverted Israel's attention from its existential problems in the region, and were intent on sabotaging the emerging peaceful relations between Israel and Saudi Arabia. Just a few days before the attack, official Israeli delegations had been invited and participated in international meetings held in Saudi Arabia.

After the massacre of the Jews on Israeli soil on October 7th, many in the Muslim countries urged the world to force Israel to accept an immediate cease fire under the mantra of avoiding a humanitarian catastrophe in the Gaza Strip. We went through this movie before. *No demands are made on Hamas, and its actions are placed "in context."* This one-sided position of the Muslim world is not by chance. The "context" was clearly stated on October 9, 2023 (barely two days after the massacre of the Jews), by Zaman Mehdi, the Pakistani Ambassador to the UN in Geneva, who – *speaking on behalf of all the 56 states of the OIC*, the Organization of Islamic Cooperation – condemned the "***more than seven decades of illegal foreign occupation, aggression***". Notice the quote: "*more than seven decades*", placing thus the root cause of the conflict in the creation of the State of Israel ***in 1948*** (and not in the occupation of the West Bank and Gaza following the 1967 war.)

Figure 8.1: The Pakistani Ambassador to the UN in Geneva, addressing the UN on October 9th, 2023 (audio-text: *"reminder of more than seven decades of illegal foreign occupation, aggression ..."* (source: X, formerly Twitter).

To this day, no one in the Arab world – nor in the "progressive" Left in the Western democracies – wants to admit the reality that half the Jewish population of Israel consists of Jewish refugees from the Arab countries, who after enduring centuries of the worst kind of oppression as "dhimmis" under Islamic rule, were ethnically cleansed from the Muslim countries during the 20th century, from Morocco, in Africa, to Iran, Iraq, and Yemen in the Middle East. *Israel was born as a nation of refugees.*

The root cause of the Arab-Israeli conflict is the opposition of the Muslim world to the right of self-determination of the Jewish people. The Muslim world still dreams about reducing the Jews back to their previous status of "dhimmis", a "tolerated" minority – at best. Or their expulsion and ethnic cleansing from their indigenous land, the Land of Israel – the only place where the Jews were able to flourish back as a people – at worst. In their minds, there is no place for an independent Jewish State in the Middle East.

Three months later …

Three months later, on January 11, 2024, South Africa repeated the same arguments presented by the Pakistani ambassador on October 9, 2023 on behalf of the Organization of Islamic Cooperation. *The conflict is not about the West Bank and Gaza. The problem is about **1948**, the existence of the State of Israel*, something that is wrong and should be reversed, by allowing the "*right of return*" of millions of Palestinians to Israel proper, within its June 1967 armistice lines, and thus, bringing an end to the Jewish State:

Open statement of South Africa to the International Court of Justice, on January 11, 2024:

Figure 8.2: Open statement of the South Africa representative to the International Court of Justice, The Hague, on January 11, 2024 (source: DW German News)

Madam President, distinguished members of the Court:

It is an honor and privilege for me to appear before you today on behalf of the Republic of South Africa. I wish to express my gratitude to the Court for convening this hearing on the earliest possible date to entertain South Africa's request for the indication of provisional measures in this matter.

In our application, South Africa has recognized the ongoing Nakba of the Palestinian people through Israel's colonization since 1948, which has systematically and forcibly dispossessed, displaced and fragmented the Palestinian people, deliberately denying them the internationally recognized and inalienable right to self-determination, and the internationally recognized right of return as refugees to their towns and villages in what is now the State of Israel.

Etc., etc., etc., …

What is Hamas – The Hamas war doctrine and objectives

(Published originally as a chapter in the first edition of my book "*Boycott of Israel is wrong: How to fight it*", on June 3, 2021, following the May 2021 conflagration between Hamas and Israel.)

In an inversion of science fiction novels where the elite class enjoys life outside on the ground while keeping the lower class working underground in inhuman conditions, Hamas' war doctrine consists of keeping the dispensable items outside in the open, while the military assets and the elite political and military cadres live and operate underground.

Dispensable items include civilians and civilian buildings and infrastructure: this is what the press and social media see and report, both during normal days and especially during armed conflicts, when emotions run high. These are *dispensable* items: they are continuously replenished and rebuilt in between armed conflicts, by natural population growth and the influx of money from Muslim states and well-meaning naïve Western European organizations. A significant part of this money is diverted to the military infrastructure, from building a complex system of underground tunnels and installations, to the development and manufacture of military equipment. As in the science fiction novels, health and material conditions of this low-class dispensable population are kept to the minimum necessary to insure the continuation of this regime and the achievement of its objectives. Ideological indoctrination is strictly imposed at the schools from a young age.

Hamas' ideology is simple and it is this simplicity that makes it so powerful to the masses: *"Israel will exist and will continue to exist until Islam will obliterate it, just as it obliterated others before it"*. This declared objective appears right at the beginning of *Hamas' Covenant*, as translated and published by the Yale University School of Law [1]

To dispel any doubts between being only *"anti-Israel"* or just plain *"antisemitic"*, Hamas' Covenant spells this explicitly*: "The Prophet, Allah bless him and grant him salvation, has said: 'The Day of Judgement will not come about until Moslems fight the Jews (killing the Jews), when the Jew will hide behind stones and trees. The stones and trees will say O Moslems, O Abdulla, there is a Jew behind me, come and kill him."*

Furthermore, if anyone still thinks that a compromise with Hamas can be achieved, here comes again Hamas' Covenant. Under the title of *"Peaceful Solutions, Initiatives and International Conferences"*, Hamas states: *"Initiatives, and so-called peaceful solutions and international conferences, are in contradiction to the principles of the Islamic Resistance Movement ... Initiatives, proposals and international conferences are all a waste of time and vain endeavors."*

Plain and simple. As were the means used to demonize the Jews by Nazi Germany and as is the demonization of Israel by the fanatic religious regime of the Ayatollahs since they took power in Iran in 1979.

These three regimes, Nazi Germany, Iran's Ayatollahs and Hamas share the same ideological structure: after clearly stating their objective (despicable as it may be) they then proceed methodically towards achieving this objective. Their reasoning does not differ in one iota from the logic used, for example, by Euclid in his Geometry: state clearly a few basic axioms and then systematically proceed to derive all their consequences. One just has to accept the premises, then anything else is logic and justifiable.

The Western media willfully ignores Hamas' ideological axioms and then hand-picks selected *"facts"*, for example, Israel's *"disproportionate"* use of force and the *"unbalanced"* number of casualties on both sides. Hamas launched its first rockets towards Jerusalem and other Israeli cities on May 10, 2021. Since then, it fired during ten days more than 3,500 rockets towards Israeli cities. In response, the Israeli air force launched hundreds of sorties. No one in the media and the press seems to notice the incongruence that after *thousands of precise and powerful guided-bombs* used by the Israeli air force only about *200 Gazans were killed*. Were these pilots all drunk and merit an *"F"* for abject failure, or is something else going on? What are these pilots targeting then?

By comparison, German civilians – men, women and children – killed by the Allied strategic bombing on Germany soil during World War II ranged between 350,000 to 500,000. Hitler committed suicide in his underground bunker on April 30, 1945, to avoid being captured alive by the advancing American and Russian forces. Only then, Nazi Germany surrendered days later on May 7, 1945.

Eliminate the State of Israel and kill Jews until they submit to Islamic rule. These are not empty slogans from a fringe group. This is an ideology deeply entrenched for centuries in the Muslim world against *non-Muslim minorities* in their midst. It is taught and inculcated to children from young age. It is clearly stated in Article 11 of the *Hamas Covenant* [1]: *the land [from the Jordan River to the Mediterranean Sea] belongs to the Umma (Islamic communities) and can never be relinquished*. The difference between Hamas in Gaza and the Palestinian Authority (PA) in the West Bank is only in the means but not in the end result. The PA – having discarded the violent path after the unsuccessful Intifadas launched in 1987 and 2000 – intends to achieve the dissolution of the State of Israel by *"non-violent"* means: all the peace initiatives between the PA and Israel failed so far because of the refusal of the PA to renounce to the *"right of return"* of *millions* of Palestinians to Israel proper. How the Jews will accept this influx of millions of migrants by *"non-violent"* means is left unexplained.

-

[1] *"Hamas Covenant 1988 – The covenant of the Islamic Resistance Movement"*, published by the Yale School of Law:

https://avalon.law.yale.edu/20th_century/hamas.asp

***

Lesson 9

The day after: Back to the 242

The day after: Israel should set sustainable objectives for Gaza

(Published in the "Times of Israel" newspaper, December 10, 2023)

No one doubts that Israel can destroy the military infrastructure of Hamas. ***This is the easy part*** (human cost left aside) – *and this objective can be mainly achieved in a few more weeks-time.*

But who will govern the Gaza Strip after the defeat of Hamas? ***Who will provide the billions of dollars needed to rehabilitate the civil infrastructure, who will provide civil governance, health, and humanitarian services to the population in Gaza afterwards?*** Will it be Israel? Will this be sustainable? The example of the US intervention in Afghanistan suggests the opposite. To get a rough idea: it is estimated that the twenty-years stay of the US in Afghanistan cost more than 2 trillion dollars to the US taxpayers.

Furthermore, whereas in Afghanistan the US enjoyed the support of part of the Afghan population, the civilian population of Gaza is not an innocent victim in this war: The Palestinians in Gaza elected Hamas in free elections in 2006. Since then, Hamas quickly eliminated any opposition to its rule, and imposed a strict ideological indoctrination from young age at the schools, to assure the continuation of this regime. As a result, Hamas enjoys today from a wide support in Gaza, especially within the young indoctrinated generation. *Does Israel want to take care for years without end of the needs of a restive population of more than two million Palestinians in Gaza?*

Israel will have already enough on its shoulders without Gaza: the rehabilitation of the destroyed towns on Israel's side of its border with Gaza, as well as the return of the tens of thousands of displaced Israelis that lived there before October 7th. And this, assumes that the situation in its northern border with Lebanon will end pacifically without a confrontation with Hezbollah, and tens of thousands of displaced Israelis in northern Israel will be able to return to their homes there. On top of this, the return of Israel to a start-up vibrant economy will require a lot of attention and resources.

What then should Israel do?

Israel's forces south of Wadi Gaza should leave once two objectives will be achieved: the destruction of the military infrastructure of Hamas and the return home of the Israeli hostages. *Israel should not seek the elimination and replacement of Hamas as a governing body south of Wadi Gaza. Israel should leave this task to the people of Gaza.* Regime change will not happen today or tomorrow: It may take a generation-time. It will happen when the Palestinians will realize the catastrophes this regime – that they elected and supported – brought upon them.

Allow the new reality to sink in the minds of the people

Genocidal movements and horrendous acts of aggression, like the one perpetuated by Hamas on October 7th on Israeli soil [1], must have consequences and these consequences must be long-term and be seen, so the people in the region internalize them, and change their behavior accordingly.

A precedent of recent history: Neither the Western Allies nor Russia thought that the German people were innocent victims of World War II, and that they were entitled to a restoration of the pre-war Germany borders, and ethnic Germans were unceremoniously expelled in the hundreds of thousands.

Nazi Germany was not offered a red carpet at the end of World War II, and neither Gaza should.

The Gaza Strip should stay divided (de-facto, if not de-jure) into its northern section (north of Wadi Gaza), under Israel's jurisdiction and its southern section (south of Wadi Gaza) under Egypt's jurisdiction. Egypt, for political reasons will probably not recognize this arrangement, but a large part of the actual burden and responsibility of any future military adventures of the Palestinian rulers south of Wadi Gaza, will actually fall on Egypt, because Egypt will control its border. Hopefully, a formal arrangement could be agreed upon to station Saudi Arabian, Jordanian and Egyptian lightly-armed forces south of Wadi Gaza.

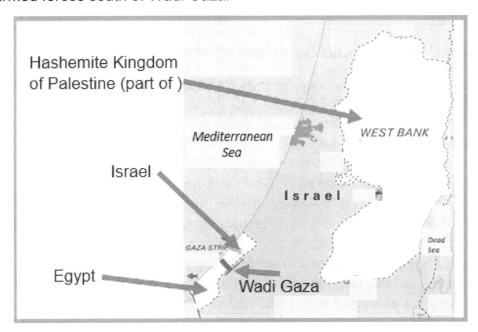

Figure 9.1: The Gaza Strip divided by Wadi Gaza between its northern and southern parts. **Lexicon:** *Wadi*: a valley or ravine that is dry except in the rainy season. (Map source: The Central Intelligence Agency of the US. Additional text and arrows added by the author)

North of Wadi Gaza

North of Wadi Gaza will be demilitarized and remain under Israeli jurisdiction. This will allow for a safe return of the large majority of the tens of thousands of presently displaced and war-traumatized Israelis to the border towns next to Gaza, and the rebuilding of their communities. Israeli civilians will not return to rebuild their lives there, after the horrible traumas they experienced on October 7th, if they do not see iron-clad basic changes on the other side of the border: the leaders of Hamas are on record of promising another "October 7th" again, and again.

South of Wadi Gaza

Israel should disconnect itself from any future responsibility of providing electricity, water, work permits and humanitarian aid to Gaza south of Wadi Gaza: It will up to the Palestinians to procure these necessities by themselves, as any other people on this planet do. Israel should not interfere with the flow of goods and people through the Rafah crossing: What comes and goes through the Rafah crossing will be for the Palestinians and Egypt alone to decide.

The Israeli policy regarding Gaza south to the Wadi Gaza should consist in the foreseeable future only on mainly defensive measures, to avoid a repetition of the territorial invasion into Israeli territory by creating effective buffer zones, or to repel any aerial attack, either using the Iron Dome or air force strikes on the sources of fire south of Wadi Gaza.

Hamas (and Iran) should be defeated strategically

The end of the major military operations in Gaza around the end of the January 2024 time frame will allow Israel and the US to concentrate on restoring the past achievements of the Abraham Accords (with the UAE, Bahrein and Morocco) and strive to achieve peace also between Israel and Saudi Arabia. I believe there will still be a short window of opportunity to achieve this, when the interests of the United States, Saudi Arabia and Israel are still aligned, and pressed by the political calendar in the US: any significant tri-lateral treaty must be approved by Congress by September 2024, before the US presidential elections in November 2024. Do not let Hamas and Iran achieve their main goal of their aggression, which was to derail this process. ***Diplomatic normalization and the establishment of peaceful relations between Israel and the largest and most important Muslim country in the Middle East can only be achieved – but not guaranteed – if the present war between Hamas, the Islamic Jihad and Israel has clear, limited, and tangible achievable objectives, and is short, decisive, and ends in a few weeks-time.***

Israel will need new elections during the Spring of 2024

Much has changed since October 7th. Many Israelis are still in shock and in pain, but once the tens of thousands of displaced Israelis in the south, near the Gaza border, and in the north, in the border with Lebanon, will return safely to their homes, Israelis will have to quickly go through a process of introspection, analyze why so many things went so wrong, and make the needed corrections to avoid a repetition of these failures.

In a democracy the tool to correct wrongs – real or perceived – is elections. Elections will enable a healthy discussion about what kind of society Israelis want for themselves and what political solutions they prefer in relation to their Arab neighbors.

These elections should be called as soon as possible: Spring 2024 would be desirable, to be consistent with the political objective of the revitalization of the Abraham Accords, and the establishment of peaceful relations between Israel and Saudi Arabia, under the auspices of the present US administration.

Hopefully, this time the Israelis will prefer a unity government based at its core on the largest secular Zionist parties, and avoid being held hostage again to small extremist factions.

Notice that in the last elections, held a year ago, in November 2022, the three major secular Zionist parties (the Likud, Yesh Atid, and the National Unity party) got a clear majority of 68 seats in the Knesset (out of 120 seats). The latest polls held just two weeks ago by the Israeli newspaper Maariv, on November 15-16, 2023, gave these three parties again an ample majority of 74 seats.

The future of the West Bank

If one could find something positive in the horrible events of October 7th, it is in that the Gordian knot tying Gaza and the West Bank, and impeding any political solution of the Arab-Israeli conflict, can be now effectively untied: The political clock for Gaza does not have to be tied to the political clock in the West Bank. Let the Palestinians in Gaza get the time to decide what future they want for themselves and their children: get rid of Hamas and live in peace with Israel, or persevere in the path of Hamas, that only brought to them one catastrophe after another.

The Oslo Accords signed in 1993 between the Palestinian Liberation Organization (PLO) and Israel were proven wrong during the Camp David meetings in 2000 between the US, the Israelis and the Palestinians [See Lesson 3]: the Palestinians saw then the Oslo Accords – and the Palestinian Authority in the West Bank of today still see them - as part of a two-stage approach: first stage, the return to the pre-1967 borders by an ephemeral creation of a 2-state solution: one state, Israel, within its pre-1967 borders, and a second state, Palestine, comprising the West Bank and Gaza. The second stage envisaged by the Palestinians is the implementation of the "right-of-return" of millions of Palestinians to Israel within its pre-1967 borders, eliminating thus, in fact, the Jewish State (how this influx of millions of Palestinians into Israel could be implemented pacifically is left unexplained by the Palestinians.)

A different approach for the West Bank is needed. Essentially, the Oslo Accords signed in 1993 between the PLO and Israel represented a sharp turn for the worse, away from the 242 UN resolution of November 1967, and led to nowhere. Israel must propose a return to the UNSC 242 resolution and negotiate with Jordan the solution to the conflict. This means, the reunification of Jordan with a demilitarized West Bank [Details are given in Lesson 7]

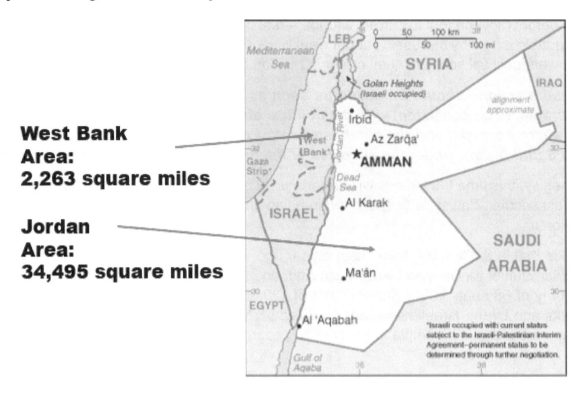

West Bank Area: 2,263 square miles

Jordan Area: 34,495 square miles

Figure 9.2: The Hashemite Kingdom of Palestine, with Jordan and the West Bank as its constitutive parts (Map source: Central Intelligence Agency, USA)

The return to the 242 UNSC resolution should also include addressing the refugee problem: Palestinian refugees and Jewish refugees, both victims of the Arab-Israeli conflict. An international aid program – similar to the Marshall Plan for Europe after World War II – should be established to develop the economy of Jordan and integrate the Palestinians in the Hashemite Kingdom of Palestine. And the international community should also address a just resolution of the claims of the almost one-million Jewish refugees, who were ethnically cleansed from the Arab countries.

Reference

[1] "'*Screams Without Words': How Hamas Weaponized Sexual Violence on Oct. 7*", by Jeffrey Gettleman, Anat Schwartz and Adam Sella, *The New York Times*, December 28, 2023

https://www.nytimes.com/2023/12/28/world/middleeast/oct-7-attacks-hamas-israel-sexual-violence.html

A true Arab Peace Initiative

(Published in the "Times of Israel" newspaper, February 18, 2024)

The **first step** in a true Arab Peace Initiative should be to **give descendants of Palestinians, who were born in the Arab countries, full citizenship rights in their countries of residence.** The wealthy Arab countries should provide all the needed help for the full integration of these refugees in their present countries of residence, including the eradication of all the refugee camps. According to the UNRWA, about 2,700,000 Arabs of Palestinian descent live today in Lebanon, Syria, and Jordan. Among them, more than 2,000,000 are in Jordan.

This is long overdue: this is an elemental recognized right for all descendants of refugees in all the other conflicts in the world: the right to rebuild their lives in their new countries of residence. The Palestinians became the exception to the rule: They were kept for generations as refugees in the Arab countries to sustain and provide a justification for the continuation of the war against the State of Israel.

Israel did its part by integrating more than half a million Jewish refugees from the Arab countries. Around half of the present Jewish population in Israel is descendent from Jewish refugees from Arab countries. It is time for the Arab states to do their part in integrating the Palestinian refugees in their countries of residence.

The **second step** in a true Arab Peace Initiative is for the Arab countries to **support the 242 United Nations Security Council resolution**. This means **support the reunification of the West Bank with Jordan.** Added rationality for the adoption of the 242, from an Arab point of view, was provided in reference [1], as well as an aptly name for the reunified state: The "*Hashemite Kingdom of Palestine*".

Following the model of the peace treaty between Egypt and Israel, the West Bank will be demilitarized (as the Sinai Peninsula is). The final recognized international borders between the State of Israel and the *Hashemite Kingdom of Palestine*, replacing the 1949 armistice line, will be decided through negotiation, but will resemble the pre-June 1967 armistice line, with some territorial swaps here and there. *No one will be forced to leave his/her home:*

No one will be forced to leave his/her home

After a recognized international border between Israel and the Hashemite Kingdom of Palestine will be established, replacing the armistice (cease-fire) lines of 1949, some small Jewish towns, presently in the West Bank, might appear within the Hashemite Kingdom of Palestine international borders. Similarly, some small Arab towns, presently in the West Bank, might appear within the international border of Israel. The same might happen with some small Arab towns presently within Israel's 1949 armistice borders: they might appear within the Hashemite Kingdom of Palestine international borders. No one will be forced to leave his/her home, and the individual civil rights of these people will be respected. This will include their rights to keep their ties with their fellow citizens on the other side of the international border. This will also include their right to hold dual-citizenship.

If these basic two steps are adopted by the Arab Peace Initiative, then – within this framework – the political future of the Gaza Strip can be resolved too. The political time line may be longer and the political future may be open to discussion. However, some principles could be established and implemented immediately. These would include: 1) The Gaza Strip will be demilitarized, 2) All the Israeli hostages will be set free, and *within (and only within) the framework of reconciliation between people*, all the Palestinians held presently in Israeli prisons will be released as well, 3) An international initiative will be launched to rehabilitate the Gaza Strip and eliminate the remaining refugee camps in the Gaza Strip.

If the Arab countries adopt this initiative, then the recognition of the Jewish State by the Arab countries, and the establishment of diplomatic, economic, and cultural relations ("peace"), will just be a simple trivial formality that will recognize the new reality on the ground.

Unfortunately, all the Arab peace initiatives that have been floated through the years and also lately, look more like a "**2-stage solution**", instead of a "**2-state solution**": First stage, the establishment of an ephemeral Palestinian state in the West Bank and Gaza; and second stage, the elimination of the State of Israel by waging "the war of return" of millions of Palestinian refugees to the State of Israel within its pre-June 1967 borders, or what all the Arab "*peace*" initiatives call, the "*achievement of a just solution to the Palestinian Refugee problem to be agreed upon in accordance with UN General Assembly Resolution 194.*" (See, for example, the Arab Peace Initiative from 2002)

There were two groups of refugees created by the long conflict between the Arab world and the Jewish people: All the Arab "peace" initiatives only recognize one.

Reference

[1] The reunification of the West Bank with Jordan, the name "**Hashemite Kingdom of Palestine**", as well as the rationality of this proposal, were explained by Ali Shihabi, a close confident of Crown Prince Mohammed Bin Salman, in the Saudi Royal Family-owned news outlet "Al-Arabiya News", in an article he published on June 8, 2022:

https://english.alarabiya.net/in-translation/2022/06/08/The-Hashemite-Kingdom-of-Palestine

End the humanitarian crisis in Gaza in 24 hours and set the parameters for peace

(Published in the "Times of Israel" newspaper, March 18 and 20, 2024)

Israel and the US should end the unnecessary frictions between them. The humanitarian crisis in Gaza can be ended in 24 hours, if Israel and the US will agree to the following:

The Gaza Strip should be de-facto partitioned

The Gaza Strip should be partitioned between a northern and southern parts, with the boundary between them being essentially Wadi Gaza. The Gaza Strip north to Wadi Gaza will be administrated by Israel. The Gaza Strip south of Wadi Gaza will continue being administrated by the Palestinians, presently Hamas.

Figure 9.3: The Gaza Strip divided by Wadi Gaza between its northern and southern parts. **Lexicon:** *Wadi*: a valley or ravine that is dry except in the rainy season. (Map source: Ocha, BBC)

The long-term Israeli control of the northern part of the Gaza Strip will allow for a safe return of the large majority of the tens of thousands of presently displaced and war-traumatized Israelis to the border towns next to northern Gaza, and the rebuilding of their communities. Israeli civilians will not return to rebuild their lives there, after the horrible traumas they experienced on October 7th, if they do not see iron-clad basic changes on the other side of the border: the leaders of Hamas are on record of promising another "October 7th" again, and again.

Humanitarian aid to Gaza South of Wadi Gaza

Israel should not interfere – nor even give the impression of such thing – with the flow of humanitarian goods through the Rafah crossing, at the border with Egypt, nor should Israel inspect them: Israel should take at face value declarations issued by recognized international aid organizations and Egypt about the contents of the humanitarian aid they provide. The flow of this humanitarian aid should only be limited by the capacity of these humanitarian organizations and Egypt to deliver it.

Humanitarian aid to Gaza North of Wadi Gaza

Israel will ensure that all the needed humanitarian aid reaches the civilian population North of Wadi Gaza. All this humanitarian aid will use terrestrial routes between Israel and northern Gaza, and will be inspected by Israel.

The above solution could be implemented immediately, ending the humanitarian crisis.

There are two objections to the immediate implementation of the above solution: on one side, the idea of a de-facto division of Gaza for years to come into a northern and southern part (similar to the division of Nazi Germany after World War II into West and East Germany) is presently an anathema for the US. On the other side, due to the massacre and atrocities committed by Hamas on October 7th, Israel has switched from a long-held perspective that a rule of Gaza by Hamas is tolerable, to a totally opposite perspective that even a temporary continuation of the rule of Hamas on any part of Gaza is intolerable. Both objections are counterproductive.

The parameters for peace

Beyond the immediate crisis, Israel and the US should set a common vision on how to solve the Arab-Israeli conflict. First, the refugee problem.

The refugee problem

There were two groups of refugees created by the Arab-Israeli conflict: the Jewish refugees from the Arab countries, and the Palestinian refugees from the 1948 Arab-Israeli war.

Any peace initiative should refer to both groups, or none of them. *This balanced approach was explicitly adopted by the US Congress:* The HR 185 Bill (year 2008) states that "*Middle East refugee resolutions which include a reference to the Palestinian refugee issue must also include a similarly explicit reference to the resolution of the issue of the Jewish refugees from Arab countries*".

This was also the approach taken by the UN Security Council in November 1967, when it approved the 242 UNSC resolution. After the US and Britain rejected the motion of the Soviet Union representative to refer in it only to the Palestinian refugees, the approved 242 resolution states instead: "*The Security Council ... affirms further the necessity ... (b) For achieving a just settlement of the refugee problem.*"

The **first step** to solve the refugee problem is for the Arab states to **give descendants of Palestinians, who were born in the Arab countries, full citizenship rights in their countries of residence.** The wealthy Arab countries should provide all the needed help for the full integration of these refugees in their present countries of residence, including the eradication of all the refugee camps. According to the UNRWA, about 2,700,000 Arabs of Palestinian descent live today in Lebanon, Syria, and Jordan. Among them, more than 2,000,000 are in Jordan.

This is long overdue: this is an elemental recognized right for all descendants of refugees in all the other conflicts in the world: the right to rebuild their lives in their new countries of residence. The Palestinians became the exception to the rule: They were kept for generations as refugees in the Arab countries to sustain and provide a justification for the continuation of the war against the State of Israel.

Israel did its part by integrating more than half a million Jewish refugees from the Arab countries. *Around half of the present Jewish population in Israel is descendent from Jewish refugees from Arab countries.* It is time for the Arab states to do their part in integrating the Palestinian refugees in their countries of residence. *The Arab countries should do this now, with no further delays.*

The second part of the shared vision of Israel and the US should be how to solve the Arab-Israeli conflict. The principles for the solution of this conflict are formulated in the 242 UNSC resolution.

The 242 UNSC resolution

The Arab countries, Israel, the US, and the international community should adopt the ***242 United Nations Security Council resolution from November 1967 as the basis for the settlement of the conflict.*** This step should begin with setting the international borders in the West Bank: As part of the 242, the West Bank will be reunified with Jordan, and remain demilitarized.

No one will be forced to leave his/her home. After a recognized international border between Israel and the reunified Jordan with the West Bank will be established, replacing the armistice (cease-fire) lines of 1949, some small Jewish and Arab towns, might appear "on the wrong side" of the international border. No one will be forced to leave his/her home, and the individual civil rights of these people will be respected. This will include their rights to keep their ties with their fellow citizens on the other side of the international border. This will also include their right to hold dual-citizenship.

In the cruel reality of the Middle East, a miniature independent state in the West Bank, 55 miles long by 40 miles wide, including also the minuscule Gaza Strip, 24 miles long by 6 miles wide (called the "Palestinian State" in the "2-state solution" approach), will become a failed state, and a fertile soil and launching pad for an irredentist movement to continue the war with Israel, or as the pro-Palestinian mobs in the European cities and at the university campuses in the US proudly chant: "*From the [Jordan] River to the [Mediterranean] Sea, Palestine will be free*". Meanwhile, many in the academic and intellectual circles in the Western world either support this call for the elimination of the State of Israel (under the lofty wording of dismantling the "settler-colonialist" enterprise), or cowardly stay silent, intimidated. Or shamelessly deceive the public, saying that this call is just a spiritual aspiration, with no actual violent genocidal connotations.

Appendix 9.1

Resolution 242 (1967) of the UNSC, 22 November 1967

The *Security Council*,

Expressing its continuing concern with the grave situation in the Middle East,

Emphasizing the inadmissibility of the acquisition of territory by war and the need to work for a just and lasting peace in which every State in the area can live in security,

Emphasizing further that all Member States in their acceptance of the Charter of the United Nations have undertaken a commitment to act in accordance with Article 2 of the Charter,

1. *Affirms* that the fulfilment of Charter principles requires the establishment of a just and lasting peace in the Middle East, which should include the application of both the following principles:

    (i)   Withdrawal of Israel armed forces from territories occupied in the recent conflict;

    (ii)   Termination of all claims of states of belligerency and respect for and acknowledgement of the sovereignty, territorial integrity and political independence of every State in the area and their right to live in peace within secure and recognized boundaries free from threats or acts of force;

2) *Affirms further* the necessity

  (a) For guaranteeing freedom of navigation through international waterways in the area;

  (b) For achieving a just settlement of the refugee problem;

  (c) For guaranteeing the territorial inviolability and political independence of every State in the area, through measures including the establishment of demilitarized zones;

3. *Requests* the Secretary-General to designate a Special Representative to proceed to the Middle East to establish and maintain contacts with the States concerned in order to promote agreement and assist efforts to achieve a peaceful and accepted settlement in accordance with the provisions and principles in this resolution;

4. *Requests* the Secretary-General to report to the Security Council on the progress of the efforts of the Special Representative as soon as possible

Adopted unanimously at the 1382nd meeting.

Reference

A must read of how the 242 came into being is found in:

https://history.state.gov/historicaldocuments/frus1964-68v19/ch4

About the author

I was born in Buenos Aires, Argentina. I got my first degree in Physics, *Licenciado en Ciencias Físicas*, from the Buenos Aries University, and my Master and PhD in Physics from the Israel Institute of Technology, "*The Technion*". In parallel with my studies in the secondary public school in Argentina, y studied and got the diploma of "Hebrew Teacher" at the "Seminar of Hebrew Teachers", the main secular secondary school of the Jewish community of Buenos Aires (localized in the second floor of the AMIA building, destroyed by a bomb in 1994).

If you would like to know more about me, please, do a simple search using Google.